THE UGLY SIDE OF BEAUTY

THE ~~UGLY~~ SIDE OF BEAUTY

RACHEL NIXON

Everything Hand Tied
www.everythinghandtied.com

The Ugly Side of Beauty
Copyright © 2025 by Rachel Nixon

Hardcover ISBN: 979-8-9924826-0-7
Paperback ISBN: 979-8-9924826-1-4
eBook ISBN: 979-8-9924826-2-1

To learn more about Rachel and Everything Hand Tied, please visit www.everythinghandtied.com.

CONTENTS

CHAPTER ONE

"I'm sorry. We are going to have to ask you to step down as a stylist with us." Ann Marie's lips pulled up in a contorted half-smile, half-frown as her brows pulled together in mock sympathy. I'm sure she thought it was a reasonable facsimile of a kind, caring expression, but anyone watching could see that she didn't actually care. She was just uncomfortable letting me go.

"You're firing me?" I asked, sitting back against my chair. I sat on one side of a table in the back room of the Hogs and Heifers salon, surrounded by the smell of coffee and styling products, with the three owners facing me from the other side of the table. "Why?"

Ann Marie spread her hands across the table and tilted her head, letting her long, blond beach waves fall across her shoulder. She opened her mouth to speak, but Rebecca put a hand on her arm, indicating that she was jumping in to ease her discomfort.

"I think, if I can interject here," Rebecca said, shooting a loaded, anxious glance at Ann Marie. Her voice held that mousy quality meant to soften the blow, but it only made her sound disingenuous. "What Ann Marie is trying to say is that the atmosphere and camaraderie of a salon is really important. We like to think of ourselves as a team, and I just don't know if...umm..."

While Rebecca and Ann Marie were shrinking back and trying their best to ease the blow, Carolyn leaned in, embracing the mean-girl persona that made her the de facto leader of the group. "Rachel, you don't fit in here," she stated bluntly.

Hearing her say it was admittedly shocking, but I couldn't say I was surprised. I walked into work every day as the only brown girl there, surrounded by white women, many bleach blond, all wearing some variation of boho chic. I could have been the best stylist there—and I probably was—and it wouldn't have mattered. I didn't fit their aesthetic. I didn't go out for drinks every night. I was the little misfit.

Not fitting in was my specialty. I hadn't followed the traditional salon stylist pipeline. While casual salon goers may not notice during their monthly visits, tradition, cliques, and popularity are of utmost importance to the high-end salon world. It expects nearly all stylists to fit a certain mold and come from a certain lifestyle.

At twelve years old, I started hair modeling, working with a man in Sacramento, California. When I wasn't modeling, I was at his salon, picking up pieces of hair and testing my self-taught color theory. My mentor waltzed around the salon praying to the color Gods and teaching me what he knew. By sixteen, I had graduated high school early and was booking appointments—under the table, of course. I still might be there, too, had my mentor not kicked me out.

"Don't stay here," he cautioned me. The words cut like a knife. But he was right. I had only ever known him and his black salon. Little did I know that the world of black hair was drastically different from the world of white hair. At his salon, women booked appointments and planned to be there all day. My mentor and I moved from one woman to the next, working and chatting. It was an experience.

From there, I went to college, got my degree in cosmetology, and had a baby. I got married, divorced, remarried, and became a stepmother to another child. I bounced from one salon to the next, waiting to feel comfortable and at home only to find Carolyns and Ann Maries at all of them. Four years prior to that backroom meeting, I joined Hogs and Heifers and had been making it work, or so I thought. But there I was, being kicked out.

"The other stylists have complained about you being unfriendly. That isn't the kind of employee we want here," Carolyn continued. I sucked in a deep breath, working hard not to betray any genuine emotions. I was in the lion's den, and the lions would eat me alive if I showed any "weakness." Carolyn tilted her head, and a smarmy smirk pulled at her lips. "Do you have anything to say for yourself?" She thought she had won.

"Yeah, I do," I said. I had no idea what was about to come out of my mouth, but I had to say something. I sat up straight, looked her in the eye with unflinching confidence (which I didn't really feel), and said, "I'm gonna open my own salon."

Carolyn's smile wilted before forming a tight, thin line, her expression emphasized by one arched, skeptical eyebrow. "Alright," she said. "Well, I guess that's that."

I stood, gathered my things from my station, and walked out the door to my car where, once in the safety of my own space, I burst into tears. I let the shaking sobs come out unfiltered. I didn't have a cent to my name. Who the hell was I kidding? I didn't have the funds to open a salon. I felt utterly defeated. The thought of picking myself up and dragging myself to another salon to put on a facade palatable to other cookie-cutter stylists felt insurmountable. In that moment, I just didn't have the energy, let alone the confidence, to do anything but cry.

In retrospect, we can look at hard moments in our lives and be thankful for the direction they led, but when you are in the thick of it, without the benefit of time, distance, and understanding, all you feel is tension and fear and worry and hurt.

Eventually, I collected myself enough to drive home. Once on the road, I called Nica. "They asked me to leave the salon," I blubbered nearly inaudibly as soon as she answered.

Nica is my person. She is the type of friend I can call in the middle of the night with a problem, and she will show up at my door, no questions asked. I walked through life surrounded by people who didn't resonate on my wavelength. Who saw me walk into the salon and gave me a little half-smile that looked friendly, but really meant, "you aren't one of us." I always felt forced to perform a more toned down, socially acceptable version of myself that felt inauthentic. But not with Nica. With her, I can be more myself than with anyone else I have ever met, save for maybe my husband and kids—but even those relationships aren't the same as the bond I have with Nica. Sometimes, all we have to do is catch each other's eye to communicate entire thoughts without a single word.

Nica and I weren't always like that. We didn't have one of those instantaneous, magical first encounters in which we knew we would be friends for life. I actually didn't think much of her when we first met. Nica walked through the door for a haircut early in my career at Hogs and Heifers. I made my usual get-to-know-you kind of banter, and I learned she owned a successful landscaping business and had given birth to a son three months earlier.

I didn't see Nica again until a year later, by pure happenstance. Another client named Pam encouraged me to join a reiki group she hosted. Pam was kind of flaky, but I was intrigued by the idea of reiki. It turned out to be one of the greatest things I've ever learned. Reiki is energy healing with the guiding principle of love without attachment, which, in its simplest terms, means to accept yourself as you are and to accept others as they are. The first day I attended the group, I recognized Nica—she happened to be a member. At first, I saw her as just another typical rich, white girl I didn't really like who came off entitled and elitist like so many other women in my life. I would never have guessed at the time that she would become my go-to person, but it just shows that life works out in strange ways sometimes.

Nica and I largely ignored each other during the reiki group, but that changed when she hired my sixteen-year-old daughter to babysit her son. She fired her nanny without much forethought and hired my daughter, mostly because she wanted someone who would work for less money and be a little more reliable. My daughter was smart and dependable and hardworking. Everything was fine…until she got into a car accident on the way to Nica's house to babysit.

Her little Toyota Yaris slipped on black ice and spun out into a tree on the side of the road. She was lucky to have walked away from it. But Nica blamed it on the insomnia medication my daughter was taking—something she knew about only because I shared it in what was supposed to be a private safe space of the reiki group.

I resented Nica's judgment of my daughter, which created tension in the reiki group. Pam, the reiki master, approached me one day to address the problem. "You have to try to reconcile with Nica for the sake of the group. The two of you carrying so much animosity into our space isn't conducive to what we are doing here."

"Then I guess Nica should have respected this space," I shot back, but I knew Pam was right. She was strange, to say the least, but I wouldn't benefit at all from the group if I walked in angry every single day. So, I texted Nica and asked her to meet for a chat. She agreed, and we met at a popular Italian restaurant for dinner.

Our friendship was formed by a trial of fire. We were ready to strangle each other's necks and never look back, but that night, over dinner, something changed. Somehow, while spitting venom and shooting daggers through tension that felt like a physical presence, we let down our guards. After unloading all our anger, we moved on to unloading all our fears, worries, pain, and hope. Each of us somehow found strength and support in a person we thought we hated.

From that moment on, Nica was one of the most important people in my life. So, when Hogs and Heifers told me to pack my shit and leave, she was the first person I told. She listened as I sobbed over the phone.

"I just can't start looking for another salon again," I said. "Finding a place that's right for me feels so hopeless." After the words came out, I knew they were true. That was the real reason I felt so upset. Hogs and Heifers wasn't some amazing salon the likes of which I would never find again. I wasn't worried that I couldn't find another space to practice in. I was great at what I did, and I would absolutely land on my feet. The problem was, I didn't want to do it again. It was absolutely exhausting trying to find a space that felt right to me. I had allowed myself to get comfortable at Hogs and Heifers. It took a lot of energy to squeeze myself into a mold that didn't quite fit, and I just didn't know if I had that kind of energy to expend all over again.

"You don't have to worry about that right now, Rachel. Focus on one moment at a time. If you try to solve every problem at once, you will get overwhelmed," Nica said. "Go to your concert tonight." She was referring to the Beyoncé concert that I had bought tickets for months in advance.

Nica was right. I had to go to the Beyoncé concert. Part of me wanted to crawl into bed and not get out for days. I felt so devastated to have to uproot my life again, to be rejected again. But I pushed myself to go home, take a shower, and find a killer outfit to wear. While getting ready, I texted the only person from the salon that mattered to me:

Happy Birthday, Rylan!

She replied right away: *Thnx :-**

I responded: *I just wanted to let you know that I'm no longer going to be working at Hogs and Heifers. I hope that doesn't affect our relationship.*

I shot off the text, pocketed my phone, and headed out to the concert. Rylan was one of the few connections I had made at Hogs and Heifers that felt genuine and worthwhile. She was a good stylist with passion and heart, and I wanted to keep in touch.

Despite my aching heart and the stress of being unemployed, I was determined to enjoy the concert. I had up-front seats for Beyoncé and Jay-Z's On the Run tour. They had been making headlines all week with Jay-Z's picture alongside a picture of an unknown blond woman. The infamous video of Beyoncé's sister attacking Jay-Z in an elevator had people swirling with questions and confusion. But in the end, there was one assumption: Jay-Z had cheated, humiliating Beyoncé, who seemed, until that point, untouchable by scandal. Suddenly, she was vulnerable, fragile.

The lights dimmed, drenching the stadium in darkness, before four words played across the giant screens on stage: THIS IS REAL LIFE. Chills ran down my spine, and goosebumps spread across my skin. Smoke filled the stage and then—Beyoncé emerged. I was close enough to see her face. It was clear that she had been going through it. The endless news cycle of Jay-Z's affair had shaken her foundation. Her face held a fierce determination despite the visible heartbreak she held back. Tears pricked my eyes as I watched her put on the best damn concert of her life, despite the turmoil behind the scenes.

A powerful realization swept through me. If Beyoncé could do it, so could I. In that moment, I borrowed from her power and strength. I didn't have a dollar to my name. I had no idea how I would pull it off, but I knew I would open my own salon. I had to. I had no excuse to not go out and live with passion and purpose.

As I reveled in the beauty of that simple, yet impossible, decision, I felt my phone buzz in my pocket. Rylan's name popped up on the screen.

"Hey!" I said, plugging one ear, trying to hear her over the overwhelming noise.

"Rachel!" Rylan said. "What happened?"

"I'm at a Beyoncé concert. Can I tell you about it tomorrow?" I asked.

"Of course," she said. "Call me tomorrow."

That small reassurance that Rylan hadn't given up on our friendship despite the drama at the salon only added to my newfound, if unsubstantiated, confidence.

I walked away from the concert that night dizzy with excitement. I had made my decision, and nothing would stop me. I went home to a quiet house. I almost woke my husband, Reco, to tell him the big news about my decision to open a salon, but I figured it would be better to see his face in the morning.

I went to sleep unemployed and at peace.

The next morning, I found Reco in the kitchen pouring two mugs of coffee. "How was the concert?" he asked.

"Amazing!" I answered.

"Are you feeling any better after what happened with Hogs and Heifers?" he asked, eyeing me tentatively. He knew it was a sensitive topic but couldn't avoid it entirely.

"I feel great! Screw that place. I have decided I am going to open my own salon," I declared, taking a slow sip of the steaming coffee.

His eyebrows rose. "Okaaay..." he said, drawing out the word. He had questions but didn't want to stifle my excitement.

My phone buzzed. "Oh, hold on. Let me grab this." I answered the phone and stepped out of the room.

"Rachel," came Rylan's voice. "Tell me what happened!" I could hear the mix of outrage and curiosity in her voice. Of course, she would have heard Carolyn's version of events, but luckily, she knew not to trust that account.

"They fired me. They told me I didn't fit in, and no one liked me, and then they fired me."

"What the fuck?" she blurted. "Those bitches!"

I laughed. There was something comforting about having someone on my side. "I'm sure it is for the best," I said.

"So, what are you going to do now?" she asked.

"I'm going to open my own salon."

"Oh, my God! How?" I could sense her incredulity without the need to see her shocked expression.

"Well..." I laughed. "I don't really know yet."

"I'm sure you will find a way," she said. We talked for a few more minutes about the salon, Carolyn, and all the drama. Then she gasped, interrupting me mid-sentence.

"What?" I asked, worried something terrible had happened on her end of the phone.

"I just had an amazing idea!" She was giddy with excitement. "You know my mom," she began. I did know her mom. She was a wonderful woman whom I had a good rapport with from her visits to the salon. "She has twenty-five thousand dollars waiting in savings for me to start my own salon. She won't give it to me until I have a reliable business partner. You could be my reliable business partner!"

Now it was my turn to gasp. It felt too good to be true. Somehow, the financial backing for my dream had just fallen into my lap. "Okay," was all I could manage to say.

After that, everything happened quickly. Rylan's mom agreed to our business venture and wrote a check to both of us for twenty-five thousand. Then, I borrowed another fifteen thousand at ten percent interest from a rich trust-fund woman in my reiki group whom Pam introduced me to. Rylan and I came up with a business name, set up an LLC and business account, and rented a space.

Butterflies took flight in my stomach as we stepped into the salon, which we named Urban Elements, for the first time. It was a beautiful, high-end salon with eight spaces on the south end of Theatre Square in downtown Sonoma where we would get plenty of foot traffic. I envisioned it as a space for community and education. Early in my career, I had been introduced to the Davines color line. At first, I didn't understand it. The method went against every color theory I had learned, but once I spent some time learning, Davines products quickly became the only products I would use. I even became the leading educator for the brand in California. Beyond styling and coloring, educating is my genuine passion. I love helping other stylists find their own visions and connect with great practices. My very own salon would be the prime place to expand on my desire to educate.

I didn't have any experience renting a space, but I had what I considered a reasonable sense of finance and business. I knew how to pull in clients. Rylan brought a great design aesthetic to our partnership, so she knew how to make the space unique and inviting, unlike other salons in the area. Before we even opened the doors, we were fully booked, with eight stylists renting out chairs.

With that, we opened our doors for business and found ourselves flooded with clients. I felt like I had landed in the *Field of Dreams* movie—if you build it, they will come. And they did. All of my dreams were falling into place, so much so that I somehow ignored all the red flags waving wildly around me.

CHAPTER TWO

"I can't pay my bills," I said, two years after opening the salon. My husband and I sat side by side on the couch after I put the kids to bed. Reco muted the TV and turned his body to face me. I couldn't hide the worry in my expression, nor did I want to. Reco, from the moment I met him, had been the solid, unshakable foundation that kept me grounded—a shocking difference from my first husband, whom I married largely to fill the space of the partner I so desperately wanted.

I hadn't been looking for a husband when I met Reco, and he never had any intention of settling down and getting married. Our upbringings, in some respects, were opposite of each other. I was raised in California by relatively affluent parents (until the shit hit the fan), and he was raised in the Lower Ninth Ward of New Orleans.

In other respects, our lived experiences had enough through lines to bring us together. We both understood what it was like to be the outcast and the black sheep. When he first brought me home to meet his parents, I received a loving and warm reception. They embraced me without any questions asked, which filled a void I didn't even know I had. Much later, I learned they thought I was white. Racial confusion was something I had been used to dealing with since elementary school when I, or more like the other kids, was old enough to realize that I was different. With a black dad and a white mom, I didn't fit clearly into either the black or the white culture—something that reared its ugly head at every salon I tried to work at. Despite Reco's family historically coming down on the side of no race mixing, they didn't bat an eye when they saw me.

As much as I liked his parents, Reco and I didn't seem meant to be. So many barriers were in our way that we should have broken up in the first year of dating. But somehow, we worked. He was a calming, grounding force to my free, untethered spirit. So, when I sat on the couch, nearly in tears over the state of my business, his no-nonsense reaction didn't surprise me.

"I'll take care of it," he said. He didn't ask questions. His face didn't betray any emotions. He simply did what he had to do. He worked at the time at a legal cannabis dispensary and, after I told him about my financial troubles, he upped his side hustle. It was a risk. We both knew it, but neither of us talked openly about it. There was no other choice.

If it had been up to me, I would have closed Urban Elements and walked away at that point. If two years earlier people had told me I would feel this way, I would have laughed in their faces and called them crazy. But there I was, ready to give up.

Our first year in business was amazing. The salon ran so smoothly; it was as if someone had looked inside my head, pulled out my wildest dreams, and turned them into reality. Our eight stations were full of stylists whom I liked and respected. We were booked all the time. When I wasn't in the salon, I was traveling all over California and the world learning new styles and techniques to bring back to my own salon. I felt like I was really doing something. I forged my path. I created an educational space for everyone who walked through the doors. I made a name for myself in the local industry.

Yet, every penny I made seemed to go right back into the business. Each month, I paid ten thousand dollars just to keep the doors open, before paying any other expenses. I had no formal training in running a business or the financial side of things, so I couldn't figure out where the hell all my money was going. I trudged home exhausted every single night without a penny to my name. But simultaneously, the salon's popularity skyrocketed.

When the business that shared a wall with us left its space, we decided to expand. It seemed like the only reasonable choice. Our stylists were always booked for weeks out. New stylists were desperate to get a spot. And I figured the added revenue of five more chairs might solve the problem of my take-home pay, or lack thereof.

So, we signed a new lease and started knocking down walls.

Early on, the familiar scents of perfumed, high-end shampoos and styling products mixed with the subtle scent of dust wafting in the air from the next-door renovations sent a thrill of excitement through me every time I walked through the door. It signified success and independence and some greater meaning.

Rylan set to work decorating with her clean, modern aesthetic while I hired a receptionist and filled the new stations. Almost overnight we went from being an eight-station salon to a thirteen-station salon. Our appointment book filled up easily, and for the first time, we were prepared for the overwhelming demand. Day after day, I showed up with a wide smile as I greeted all the stylists; cut, colored, and styled hair; and cut the checks.

But once the dust settled, plastering a smile on my face took more and more effort. My perspective changed as I realized the expansion was not solving my cash-flow problem as anticipated. I couldn't let anyone know the struggles behind the scenes. Even in what I would consider a great working environment like my salon, the gossip train still worked overtime. If I let anything slip, the entire world would soon know we were struggling financially, which would damage our reputation. So, I acted normally, but behind the scenes, I was stressed that finances had not gotten better. We were bringing in more money than before, so I expected to see a windfall, an increase in cash flow—something, anything. Our bills, of course, increased with the renovation, but with the extra clients and money, I shouldn't have felt like I was drowning every time I opened a bill or wrote a check.

I was working harder and longer than I had ever worked in my life. I felt like I was never home. When I wasn't at the salon as a stylist, I was at the salon as a business manager, trying to keep all the plates spinning.

"Morning, Rachel," Rylan said, shaking her iced latte before taking a sip. I looked at the clock over the door. Ten a.m.

"Morning," I said with a thin grin. It was all I could muster. The other ladies at the salon received my full, brilliant, hundred-watt smile, but I couldn't seem to pull out that kind of enthusiasm for Rylan. I watched from the corner of my eye as she moved from station to station, greeting each girl, chatting with customers, and showing off her new sweater that matched her new purse.

Finally, she set down her things and checked the schedule. A sinking feeling settled in my stomach as I watched her. One I couldn't pinpoint. She was so unconcerned. I wondered if she ever looked at the books. Did she have any idea how much rent was? Or how much debt we had from the renovations? From the beginning, I had played the part of money manager while Rylan had been along for the ride, but even so, I couldn't believe how little she seemed to care.

That afternoon, I left the salon and went straight to a reiki session with Nica, which I often did when I was spiraling down into the depth of my emotions. Reiki sessions are a double-edged sword because they help me feel instantly calmer, while at the same time they dredge up all kinds of latent emotions that I then have to reckon with over the next several days.

As expected, after the session, I felt better, calmer, and more level-headed. I got a good night's sleep and could see Rylan with a fresh perspective. The reiki had restored my hope in the future and my faith in my ability to manage the salon.

My positive attitude did not last. Over the next year, the world crept back in, and I was left going through the motions, not sleeping at night, and crying every time I looked at our financials. I had nothing to show for all of my work, and I just wanted out. But there was no out. All I could do was turn to my husband to continue paying our bills.

I didn't know the end game. I just knew that I couldn't get out of the lease, I couldn't stop paying bills, and I couldn't walk away. I lost sleep, wondering how my dream had turned so quickly into a nightmare. But more than that, I wondered how a successful business could somehow net zero actual money.

I would lie awake at night, staring at the ceiling, running through my non-existent options and replaying how the hell I had gotten there.

My life until that point had been anything but easy. I spent the majority of it desperate to fit in but lacking an identity that felt right. I could pass as black or white depending on my mood, but I wasn't accepted as either. When I was thirteen, my father left my mom, and what I had considered a mostly solid life fell out from under me. My father had been the person who always had my back, despite his drug addiction (which I didn't learn about until later). When he left my younger brother and me with our mom, he was really leaving us alone. Sure, she was technically around, but she always absent—working, dating, doing who knows what.

So, from the age of thirteen, I was left to fend for myself. I had to play the role of mother to myself and my brother. When I got older, I lost myself to wild years of partying too hard, but when I crawled out on the other side, with a newborn in my arms, I slowly pieced myself back together. I discovered a genuine sense of purpose defined by helping others.

Some people go to a salon, drop their money, get their hair cut, and don't think twice about it. For me, getting my hair styled meant so much more than that. I still believe our appearance defines us. It can bring confidence, joy, happiness, and, above all, a sense of self. My passion for hair led to education, first for myself. I wanted to know everything there was to know about hair, coloring, and styling. Through that journey, I realized how powerful helping other stylists is as well.

Traveling from salon to salon, trying to find a space I fit in, left me scrambling. I was confident, don't get me wrong; but it got harder and harder to maintain a tough exterior when everywhere I went people tried to cut me down. Was it me or the salon culture? When I finally got my own salon, I thought the struggle would be resolved. I would be free to create my own culture. To set expectations. To explore my ideas and identity.

As I lay in bed worrying those nights, my thoughts went beyond the finances. I couldn't help wondering what my struggling business said about me and about my purpose and passion.

"Do you think there is something up with Rylan?" I asked Nica over coffee one day. She had no experience in the hair industry, but she understood business. When I first told Nica about the struggling salon, I was embarrassed, but in usual Nica fashion, she hadn't been at all concerned. I was hesitant to bring up Rylan's part in all of it. If I was managing the business side of things, then wasn't it my fault we were struggling?

"Like what?" she asked.

"I don't know. She just seems so totally unconcerned."

"Do you think she knows the salon is struggling?"

"How could she not?" It seemed like the most obvious thing in the world. It consumed my every waking moment.

"I think you are going to have to have an actual conversation with her at some point."

"Do I have to?" I joked. Nica just laughed and nudged me. I usually had no problem confronting people, but in this case, I really wanted to stick my head in the sand. If Rylan didn't know what bad financial shape we were in, I was hesitant to tell her. I didn't want her to blame me.

Despite my misgivings, after that conversation with Reco, I pressed on, letting him pay the bills as I continued to work my tail off with no end in sight. To his credit, he never said a word. He never questioned me once. He just silently propped up my dream—until one day during the holiday season.

For parents, Christmas is the worst time for financial struggles. That year, though we would never let our children go without gifts under the tree, behind the scenes, tensions were high. I could feel a shift in Reco as we walked through the Nike store, brushing through the crowds, burdened with full shopping bags, as we tried to check off my daughter's list. He was a stoic sort of guy. Very little outwardly affected his emotions. On our wedding day, the officiant asked if he was a robot when he stood there solid, unmoved, and unemotional. He had emotions, but he kept them thoroughly in check. So, seeing the tension as he clenched his jaw and the tightness in his shoulders sent tendrils of worry through my thoughts.

"What is going on?" I asked finally, when we were hidden behind a rack of clothes.

He looked at me for a long moment, debating internally if he wanted to say anything. "You are stealing from the salon," he finally said.

CHAPTER THREE

I blinked and staggered as if he had physically pushed me. My mouth opened and closed, trying to form words to respond.

"I have been risking everything to help you keep the business afloat, and you are pocketing money behind my back," he whisper-shouted, looking around to make sure we weren't drawing attention. "You have been bullshitting me this entire time. You made me look like an asshole in front of Jim."

My head spun as I tried to keep up with what he was saying. Jim was Rylan's husband, and I couldn't figure out what he had to do with anything or why on earth my husband thought I was stealing from the business that I was fighting tooth and nail to keep.

"Reco, I'm not stealing from the business," I said.

"That's not what your books say," he countered. His face was still deceptively calm, despite the roiling anger beneath the surface.

"You went through my finances?" I asked. I wasn't upset. It just hurt that he felt the need to go behind my back. That he didn't come to me as soon as he started questioning things.

"Jim called me the other night," Reco said. "He told me that Rylan can't make ends meet, either. She isn't contributing to their household and can't keep up with her bills."

I couldn't say I was surprised to hear that. After all, if I was struggling in the way I was, it stood to reason that she would be too. "Okay," I said, waiting for him to continue. He didn't take his eyes off me the entire time we talked, as if he was trying to figure out who the stranger who stood before him was.

"We thought it would be best to look at the records," he said. "Rachel, there are hundreds of thousands of dollars unaccounted for."

For the second time in a matter of minutes, I felt as if a fist wrapped tightly around my lungs, and I couldn't take a breath. "What?" I said when I finally recovered. "How is that possible? Where is that money?" My mind reeled as I started imagining everything I could do with that kind of money, not the least of which was pay my damn bills.

"That is the question, Rachel," he said. "Have you been lying to me this whole time?"

"Of course not," I said. "Why would I willingly choose to live like this? All I want is for the salon to succeed. I feel like a failure not being able to pay my bills."

He softened slightly at that. I could see the tension ease from his shoulders as his eyes seemed to see the woman he married again. "I think we all need to sit down and look at the books and figure out where the hell the money is going," he said.

The next night, I poured a glass of wine at my dining room table where Rylan, Jim, Reco, and I all sat with printouts and laptops in front of us. I passed the glass to Rylan before taking a seat and sipping my own.

"We all know that there is money unaccounted for," Reco began. It wasn't his business, or Jim's for that matter, but they both had a vested interest, given the money they were spending to support us. "The question is, where is it going?"

Silence stretched uncomfortably as we took turns looking at each other and looking away. Rylan picked at a scratch on the table that was apparently fascinating enough to draw all of her focus.

"This is crazy. I know that I am not taking that money. I am not bringing any money home, for that matter. It costs us ten grand just to open the doors every day. Rylan, what is going on?" I snapped at my partner.

"I don't know why you are blaming me. I was never meant to be on the business side of things," she said too defensively.

"You can't just throw up your hands and pass off all responsibility! We are both equally invested in the salon's success. Why don't you seem to give a shit?" I asked.

"I give a shit!" she shouted at me from across the table. Her husband pleaded with his eyes for her to calm down. "I just don't know where the money is going!"

"Then who does? I bring in two hundred thousand a year, but every cent goes right back to the salon," I said. I watched her, studying the subtle way she cast her glance downward, avoiding direct eye contact with me or anyone else at the table. "If you have so little money, where did you get the three-hundred-dollar sweater you were showing off?"

She looked up sharply, her eyes squinted into a glare. She opened her mouth to defend herself, but Jim cut her off before she could. "Rylan," he said.

She sighed and sat back against the chair. "I have been taking some money, but just when I need it."

"Are you kidding me?" I said at the same time that Jim gasped, "Rylan! You've been lying?"

The tension in the room quickly felt suffocating, with Reco being the only one not on the verge of shouting or storming off. I felt utterly betrayed, and if his face was any indication, Jim felt the same way. I wanted to be done. I wanted to get up, walk away from that table, and never look back.

"I just can't believe you would jeopardize the salon like that," I said.

"Oh, relax. I'm not jeopardizing the salon. I just, you know, I just needed a little extra here and there for that course I was taking. You always say how important education is," she replied.

"Don't blame me for your deception," I said. "You have spent our money, our profits, on frivolous purchases since day one. How much did you take?"

She looked down at the table again. "I'm not sure," she shrugged.

"Looks like it was about sixty thousand the first year and a hundred and twenty thousand the next," Reco reported.

My jaw dropped to the table. "What?" I shouted. Reco put a hand on my shoulder to keep me from really losing my cool.

"At this point, I think we need to discuss solutions," Reco said calmly. "Rylan has been pulling money from the salon for two years now, while we have been struggling to make ends meet at home and at the salon. Rachel has never taken any of her paycheck home; she has put it all back in to the business to keep the doors open. Obviously, Rylan needs to stop stealing, and the books need to be balanced. Going forward, I think it's reasonable to remove Rylan's access to the salon's bank account, so she can no longer write herself paychecks, and for Rachel to take a turn bringing some money home."

I nodded my agreement while Rylan looked at Jim, gauging his reaction. When he started nodding, she shook her head. "But how does that help the business?"

"I deserve to be able to keep my paycheck, Rylan, but I would never take so much that I couldn't keep the company afloat. You have been stealing, and *now* you are suddenly concerned about the well-being of our salon?" I asked incredulously. At that moment, I promised myself that I would get out as soon as possible, but I didn't see even a glimmer of hope for that. Rylan had just as much invested in the salon as I did, even if you couldn't tell from her choices.

When they finally left, I felt exhausted. I was relieved that we had figured out and mostly resolved the finance issue. On the other hand, I felt like I would be walking into work with the enemy the next morning. Worse than that, though, I felt a little lost. In my core, I knew who I was. I knew what I was about. I felt confident in my skills and my passions, but I lacked a long-term plan. To foster my personal growth, I had been signing up for every class I could, but with Rylan at the salon, I felt there was a cap on how much I could develop. The situation left me in a difficult place that I couldn't see a way out of.

I did what I always did in those days when I needed a reset. I got on a plane headed for New Orleans, my happy place. As soon as we touched down, my stress and overwhelm settled. The feel of the air, the people, the atmosphere…it all grounded me as I walked the levee of the Lower Ninth Ward. I always imagined my life would be complete so long as I died in New Orleans.

When I went back to work, I felt restored again. I was free to focus on Urban Elements without worrying, at least for the time being, about money. I had more mental space so was more open to the possibility of new opportunities.

"Hey, Rache," Laurie said when I stepped into the break-room for my lunch. She was a stylist who had been with us since the opening of the salon. "I came across something that I thought you might be interested in."

"Oh, yeah?" I asked, pulling out a chair and taking a seat beside her.

"Well, you know how you have been looking into extensions?" she asked.

I nodded. It was true. I had been interested in extensions for a long time, but I had never offered them myself for two reasons. The first was my lack of experience and expertise. I wouldn't provide extensions for clients if I didn't feel I was the best possible person to do them. The second reason was I hadn't found a method for attaching them that resonated with me.

Since the development and rise in popularity of hair extensions in the 1960s, countless methods for attaching them, some better than others, had been pushed onto unwitting people. In the black community, women statistically go to salons more often than in the white community. A lot of black women started using extensions to protect their hair from sun, heat, and over-manipulation. Others wanted to experiment with different looks and textures. Soon, hair extensions became a staple among all demographics, but the early methods for attaching extensions could be extremely damaging to the finer, oilier texture typical of white women's hair. In the 1980s, some salons started attaching extensions with hot wax, which meant white women could more safely participate, but the extensions didn't last long. Since then, more and more techniques had come on the market. I had been keeping an eye out for a technique I wanted to learn and study, but I hadn't found anything yet. The most current and popular method involved tape and glue, which I just couldn't get behind. It was messy and not great for the hair.

"There is a new group doing extensions using what they call the hand-tied method," Laurie continued. "You gotta check them out on Instagram. They're called Style."

"Style," I muttered as I typed into Instagram. "Okay, I'll check them out."

The rest of the day, I spent all of my breaks scrolling Instagram, studying Style and everyone who worked with them. I was left feeling underwhelmed. All the pictures I came across were of cookie-cutter white women who were indistinguishable from the others. It reminded me of Hogs and Heifers. Style's clientele looked like they could all be stars on *The Real Housewives of Beverly Hills*. Nothing I read or saw spoke to me as being genuine. I had the sinking feeling I wouldn't fit in there, and I had learned never to ignore that kind of feeling.

When I got home, I sat with my computer on my lap and a glass of wine in my hand while Reco searched Netflix. Style clearly wasn't for me, but the idea of hand-tied extensions piqued my curiosity, so I Googled it. One of the first hits was NTR, Natural Threaded Rows. As I scrolled through their social media, I knew I wouldn't be content until I had explored more.

CHAPTER FOUR

When I first pulled up NTR's Instagram, I came face to face with the owner, Betty Kelleher. I almost scrolled away immediately. She was another cookie-cutter blond woman whose gaze staring from the picture looked about as empty as a flat tire. My thumb hovered over the small X in the corner, prepared to head back to the next company on my Google search, but I hesitated. I owed it to myself to scroll past the first image. The next several images were more of the same. The hair looked great, but I worried NTR was another company like all the other companies I had found in the beauty world.

And then, I landed on a video of the owner's husband talking. If I had passed him on the street, I wouldn't have given him a second thought. He looked plain, dressed in a nice suit. But when he spoke, he garnered attention. He was passionate and charismatic. He reminded me of one of those 1980s evangelical pastors I used to see while flipping through channels late at night, each promising to save your soul. And that is exactly what his message felt like—a promise to save my soul. He seemed to speak directly to me, hitting every pain point like an expert surgeon with a scalpel. He talked about freedom from money, being your own boss, untethering from the rat race, having the lifestyle you want, and getting and maintaining the clientele to afford it. He promised a high-ticket tool that would essentially change my life.

I must have watched the short two-minute video play on repeat five or six times, as a burning desire grew in my chest. This was it. I knew it. I had found the thing that would elevate my salon and my work to the next level. No more struggling to pay the bills. No more worry about filling my salon chair. No more endless hours.

My fingers fumbled as I rushed to navigate to their website to sign up. They were hosting a three-day event at the Ritz Carlton of Moon Bay. My breath caught in my throat when I read that. For as long as I had been with Reco, we had driven past the Ritz Carlton with longing, dreaming of one day getting a chance to stay there, knowing it was well outside our budget. The itinerary for the trip, while not specifically delineated on the website, included all kinds of posh luxury along with education on marketing and the NTR method. I pulled out my wallet and was ready to book it until I saw the price.

I nearly choked on my wine. I had done a lot of education courses and trips in my career, but never had I seen a price tag like these two were asking for. We had just figured out where all the money from the salon was going and hadn't yet started climbing out of the hole Rylan dug for us. Reco was still working on the side to bring in more money just to keep us afloat. I stared at that page so long that my eyes burned. I rubbed the palms of my hand together, credit card still clutched between my fingers. I knew I couldn't justify spending the money right now, but I also knew that I couldn't justify not going to the convention. If going meant that our finances could change overnight, then I had to. Being able to provide an exclusive, high-end service would change my entire business model.

So, I took a deep breath, gulped my wine, and typed in my card number. My palms felt sweaty as I confirmed the purchase. I wouldn't know if I had made the right decision until I got to the conference, learned the technique, and started offering it in my salon. But part of me knew that the NTR extension method was the thing, the missing piece I had been searching for without even knowing it. When the transaction was complete, I closed my laptop and walked away to catch my breath. It was done. No point in spinning endlessly around the "what ifs."

I told Reco, and as I expected, he was calm, cool, and supportive. He understood how my business worked. The more skills I had, the more services I could provide and the more money I could charge. In truth, it was more than that, though. Of course, I wanted to provide the best quality services to my clients, but I also desperately wanted to know how to market myself in today's world. I needed high-end sales funnels for the type of clientele and lifestyle I wanted to transition to. We had a flood of clients using our general services, but they found me through word of mouth or by searching salons and reading our positive reviews. It felt very passive. I was sick to death of being passive. I wanted to learn how to find and pull in high-end extension clients. The NTR seminar offered the chance for action.

Shortly after submitting my payment, I received a pre-training video. It showed the extension technique but didn't speak to the marketing piece at all. I practiced what I could, but all I wanted was to get to the actual event.

One month later, I packed my bag, kissed my kids good-bye, and headed for the Ritz Carlton. As soon as I stepped through the doors of the resort, the outside world faded away. I was transported to a private paradise. Worrying about anything while inside those walls was impossible. The resort was situated directly on Laguna Beach with its clear blue waters and warm white sand.

As soon as I checked in, I was given a packet with instructions. My eyes grew wide as I read through the expectations. I felt like I had been dropped into a military academy. We were expected to wear all black from head to toe to get into the NTR mindset. We had to memorize seven core principles and recite them to be let in the door of the first session. A strict schedule outlined when we were expected to wake, eat, arrive, and sleep. It didn't sound like a vacation at all. I started memorizing the seven core values as soon as I stepped onto the elevator. I reminded myself that I wasn't there to party or relax. I was there to change my life.

I fell in line quickly, soon appreciating the strict rules. The unwavering guidelines made the seminar feel more serious, more momentous, more life-altering than if I had simply soaked up the sun on the beach and showed up to a conference every so often. Every little decision was made for me, leading me toward a greater opportunity.

By the time the first session was to start, I felt pretty confident in my ability to recite the seven values. I made my way to the conference room, where a line formed outside. NTR wanted to maintain an exclusive feel, so I was one of only about ten other people. Each person stepped up to the front of the line and repeated the seven sentences we were told to memorize. Some were asked to step aside as they hadn't accurately recited them; others were waved through. When it was my turn, I quickly began repeating the lines before I lost my nerve. Without a word, the woman waved me in.

The conference room was more like an auditorium, with a stage in front, rows of seating, and a wall of ocean-view windows. I took a seat toward the front and introduced myself to the people around me. The crowd was more diverse than I had been expecting after my recent forays into extensions and the beauty industry.

The presentation began with Betty Kelleher stepping onto the stage. The group cheered, and she waved before speaking into the microphone. I watched her lay her story bare up on that stage, showing her vulnerability. She had been stuck in a bad marriage with a cheater and a fraud. She depended on her husband financially, who tightly controlled the purse strings. She wanted a way to not only be financially independent but also live a life she felt she deserved. That sounded pretty familiar to me. Instead of divorcing, she and her husband worked on their marriage and learned to love and respect each other. Through it all, they built a business together.

After Betty finished her story to a resounding round of applause, her husband, Christopher Kelleher, took the stage. He was all charisma and energy, capturing my attention the same way he had on the brief Instagram reel I had watched. He spoke like a preacher during Sunday service, telling me everything I needed to hear. I blinked away tears as all of my own pain resurfaced, all the setbacks in following my passion, all of my financial hardships and uncertainty. He laid it all out on the table as if he were telling my own story.

I was hooked.

Once every single one of us was captivated and convinced we had found our saviors, Betty and Christopher delved into the practical details. Of course, they taught us their method of attaching extensions that weekend, but more than that, they taught us how to market, which was a big reason I was there. I knew hair. I knew I could pick up the method they were teaching me. But what I really wanted to know was how to present myself as an expert and bring in clients. Their philosophy revolved around a mindset shift, to see myself as the prize rather than the viewing the client as the prize. That alone felt worth the money it had cost to get me there. I found myself nodding along as they spoke, as my enthusiasm for my craft reignited all over again. I walked away from that conference trusting myself for the first time since—well, since forever.

When all the presentations ended, I sat at the ocean-front bar, ordered a glass of wine, and watched as the sun lit the sky on fire with orange, red, and purple as it dipped beneath the horizon. I took a deep breath and felt my whole body relax. For the first time after two years of unbelievable struggle, I felt like I was breathing freely without the dark cloud of stress hovering over me.

"This is what I want," I thought. "And I'm going to get it."

CHAPTER FIVE

I went back home feeling like a new woman, as cliché as that may sound. I felt rejuvenated, re-energized, and excited. I had new extensions and marketing skills. I had a new direction that I hadn't had before and a way to get there.

I didn't waste any time. I started applying the marketing techniques I learned and bringing in new clients. Within days, I had remodeled my entire business practice. I no longer took appointments for anything other than color and extensions, and my chair was always booked, for weeks at a time. I could charge a premium for my service. Suddenly, I was breathing more easily and sleeping through the night and not wondering how the hell I would pay my bills.

I felt unstoppable. No amount of drama with Rylan could bring me down. I even paid to have another stylist NTR-certified because I had more clients than I could possibly work with.

To maintain my certification in the NTR technique, I had to pay a monthly fee. After my wonderful experience at the three-day conference and the massive growth in business I'd experienced since, I didn't hesitate to lay down five hundred dollars a month for continuing education.

Every Wednesday at noon, Betty or another higher-up in the program went live. The first Wednesday after leaving the conference, I blocked out my schedule and excitedly logged on from my laptop in the salon's back room. It had been only a week since the seminar, but I was feeling the success and hungry for anything they wanted to give me.

When my Zoom box popped up, I saw myself alongside several other women I had met at the conference as well as several unfamiliar faces. I introduced myself to the group while we waited for the presentation to start. Finally, Betty arrived on the screen, her thousand-watt smile and brilliant blond hair momentarily blinding me.

"Good afternoon, ladies!" she waved into the camera. "Today, for the hot seat, we have Tiffany. Let's all give her a warm welcome." Betty led the applause while a box showing another woman popped onto the screen. I clapped my hands while studying the faces of the others, trying to figure out what was going on. "Hot seat" sounded like an interrogation or something. Who was Tiffany, and why was she in the hot seat? Was this the continued education?

"Hi, ladies," Tiffany said, waving both her hands toward the camera. "Thanks, Betty, for the opportunity to be in the hot seat."

"Of course! We are happy to have you. Tell us what you want to talk about today," Betty said. I still didn't know what was going on. Was Tiffany some sort of expert? I hadn't seen her at the conference. I decided to take a deep breath and see where it all went.

"Well, I have just been really struggling. Like, I want to focus on my business and build, you know, my customer base, but my husband owes me $6,132.87," Tiffany began.

Okay, I know I said I was going to give this a chance, but what? I zoned out for a minute, trying to piece together what this presentation was about. When I refocused on Tiffany, tears were streaming down her face, and she seemed to have forgotten her audience altogether as she rambled on and on about the $6,132.87 that her husband owed her. I couldn't even pick up on why her husband owed her that money or if they were still together, but by the end of the one hour "presentation," I had heard her say $6,132.87 so many times that I was ready to give her the damn money just to shut her up.

Betty responded to Tiffany's sob story like a therapist, trying to redirect Tiffany's energy, telling her to work on her business. The whole thing, I guessed, was supposed to be a cathartic learning experience for all of us.

"Well, that is our time. Thank you so much, Tiffany, for sharing. Remember, ladies, if you would like to participate in the hot seat, fill out the form on the member portal of our website. We will see you all next week!"

People waved their goodbyes, and I was left blinking at a dark screen asking me to rate the quality of the call. What the hell had I just watched? I pulled up the website and scanned through all the information until I found the hot seat request form. It explained that the hot seat was part of NTR's continued education in which anyone who participated in the monthly program, anyone at all, could request to be on and talk about anything they wanted. In other words, the hot seat speakers were random NTR members, not experts in the field who could teach us techniques, marketing tips, and other things that might be worth the five hundred dollars a month I was paying for continuing education.

I shook my head and closed my laptop. "Stop being so critical," I whispered to myself before stepping out into the salon to greet my next customer. The method was working. The marketing was working. I was meeting all kinds of new people. It didn't matter that the hot seat felt like nonsense. Any unstructured session like that would be a hit or a miss; they were just trying to build a community, which was something I had been looking for all along.

After consulting with my new client, I got to work, adding extensions to her hair. Already, my fingers moved with a familiar muscle memory as my mind spun on the hot seat, Betty, the method, and the program. It was still early days, so I couldn't be certain, but I felt the tides of my life shifting. I felt like this moment was a turning point. So often, in the moment, you have no idea that certain events and choices will lead to a whole new path in your life, but this time, I felt it. I was seeing it firsthand. Urban Elements was booming. I was doing what I loved.

And yet, a nagging voice persisted in the back of my head. Not the least of my concern was Betty's consistent message to get rid of clients after eighteen months. I heard it said it at the conference multiple times, and Tiffany had even mentioned it in passing during her hot seat.

I had spent my career developing long-term, personal relationships with my clients. I prided myself on it, in fact. In black salons, customers didn't just book an appointment, show up on time, get their hair done, and leave. Women blocked off their entire days, arriving at nine a.m. and staying until closing. Getting your hair done was an event. I saw my clients in much the same way. Although they didn't stay all day, my goal was to keep them their whole lives. I wanted to be the person they thought of when they needed anything done. I couldn't possibly get rid of them after eighteen months, and I couldn't figure out why the hell I would want to.

No one ever asked Betty real, hard-hitting questions, and when the line of conversation steered toward the eighteen-month rule, she expertly avoided, deflected, and redirected. She would talk about pulling in as many customers as possible, as if new customers are better than returning customers. It was still a great program, I told myself. No one program or method was ever going to be perfect. I could take what felt right to me and ignore the rest. Betty wasn't here watching over my shoulder to nitpick my decisions.

Regardless of my doubts, which I easily brushed aside, I participated in every learning opportunity NTR offered. I had already experienced success, and all I wanted was to continue to grow. I wanted to position myself toward that multimillion-dollar business. I watched the people around me, people I respected and liked, making money hand over fist, getting out of debt, and living my dream. I learned about marketing funnels, something I had never heard of before. I learned about client acquisition and social media and money management. I threw myself into it, knowing that I was on the right path. This was it.

After several months, the masterminds and workshops started to feel repetitive. The hot seat topics were random and rarely helpful. A lot of women talked about their successes with the method and marketing. Others talked about their finances or the struggles of implementing the things they learned. Still others, like Tiffany from the first hot seat I watched, simply unloaded their own personal dramas. I didn't stop going to the hot seat sessions, but I knew I needed to up my game. Betty offered a shadowing opportunity, in which select women in the program could follow her around for two days. The idea was that you could watch the true master at work. It was time for me to apply.

If I was being honest with myself, I didn't care for Betty. After watching her for several months during the hot seat Zoom calls, I found her to be self-important, vapid, and grating. I had the nagging feeling that she was in the whole thing only for the money. I guess that should have been obvious given she opened every presentation talking about wanting to find a way toward financial independence. But I wanted that too. It made sense early on that both things could be true. I could want the freedom that money brings but also have a deeper passion about what I was trying to do.

I desperately wanted to grow my business and earn those big bucks, but this whole thing—the salon, the clients, the extensions, the business—meant so much more to me than that. My dream of success and my desire to learn and help people had become such an integral part of my identity that it couldn't possibly be unentwined. This was not a get-rich-quick scheme for me.

When I was young, I lived a reasonably normal, middle-class life (at least as far as I knew), but I lacked something that seemed to be built in for other kids. Other kids seemed to know exactly who they were and how they fit into the world and the culture both locally and at large. I never had that. I was either the black girl at the white school or the white girl at the black school.

Early on, it didn't much bother me. I didn't know enough to recognize that it should. I was just Rachel, and that was enough. Until one day, my grandmother, meaning well, sat me down in front of a mirror and said, "Look at that," pointing to my reflection in the mirror. "Rachel, you're the most beautiful girl. All the white women wish they looked like you, and so do all the black women."

While I call her grandmother, she was actually my father's aunt who raised him from six months old when his mother died. I have only two solid memories of her: her telling me I was more beautiful than the darker-skinned girls, and her going over each part of my skin, cataloging my beauty. It felt great to be called beautiful. Who doesn't appreciate a compliment? But she only ever recognized my external beauty, and, possibly, she thought I was beautiful only because I had lighter skin than she did; in her mind, light skin equated to beauty.

After looking at myself in the mirror with my grandmother that day, I left the house feeling amazing, head held high as I skipped down the sidewalk where my friends waited for me. After they finished greeting me, I announced proudly, "My grandma said I am the prettiest girl and that you all wish you looked like me." At seven, I was just as naïve as you might expect. I thought I was sharing some wonderful news with my friends, something they would be so happy about for me. We would all ooh and ahh and embrace and then go on with our day.

The first punch hit me square in the gut, and I doubled over in confusion and pain. The kicks and punches kept coming one after the next until I was convinced they would never stop. Finally, when they let up, I found myself curled into a ball on the ground, blood dripping from countless cuts, feeling like I could never stand up again. "Now you are black and blue and dirty. You are no better than us," one of them shouted before running off.

Somehow, I found my way home that day, but I was a changed person. I had gained a new perspective on the world while, at the same time, had lost a sense of myself. I stayed lost for a long, long time, drifting from one identity to the next until I picked up that first scrap of hair off my mentor's floor and tested my first color theory. Getting a job modeling for and learning from my mentor came when I desperately needed it, and the experience informed much of my identity. Growing my business was personal to me.

I wouldn't learn this lesson until much later in my journey, but the extension world ended up being a larger, higher-stakes macrocosm of that sidewalk fight. Everyone smiled pleasantly so long as we all put on our happy, Stepford-wife faces, and no one acknowledged our differences. But they were all too happy to cut each other down at the first sign of hubris or weakness.

So, I had my doubts about what I might learn from Betty, but at the very least, she might help me network and open some doors. Shadowing her was the next logical step in my education with NTR, so I filled out the request to watch her work for two days and prepared to drop another ten thousand dollars. I had already given them at least ten grand by that point. It's the cost of learning, I told myself.

I waited several days, checking my email every couple of minutes for a response to my request. I closed it with disappointment so many times that I was starting to worry the form hadn't gone through. Maybe there had been some kind of technical error that prevented my application from being delivered.

When a response finally arrived in my inbox, a nervous thrill went through my body. This was it. The next step. Forward movement.

Dear Rachel,
Thank you for your interest in shadowing Betty.
Unfortunately, your application has not been accepted. Please continue your education with Natural Threaded Rows.

Thank you,
NTR Team

It was a form letter. She had rejected me and couldn't even be bothered to tell me why. I spent the next several minutes spiraling down a bottomless pit of worry and self-doubt. How could I continue growing if I couldn't shadow Betty? Was there something wrong with me? Why had she rejected my application? Somehow my money wasn't good enough for her?

I shook my head to dislodge those kinds of thoughts. This was just more proof that Betty might be a fraud. For the first time, I really started questioning if I was on the right path. Had I made the right choice? Followed the right leader? Joined the right program? But I had come so far. I had invested eight months and thousands of dollars; I couldn't turn back on it at that point, even if Betty was a flake.

CHAPTER SIX

Walking into another convention in November, eight months after the start of my whirlwind NTR journey, felt different than I thought it would. From the moment I had first seen Christopher Kelleher give his speech, I had been all in, hook, line, and sinker. Now, Betty's rejection and the unhelpful monthly "education" sessions clouded my experience. Twice a year, NTR had conventions much like the first conference I attended, but only for certified NTR stylists. The conferences were a place for us to gather and talk shop, take classes, listen to presentations, and build a community. Of course, there was no way I would miss it, but it just felt different in ways I couldn't exactly pinpoint.

"Welcome, ladies!" Betty shouted into the microphone as we all milled around the conference room with drinks in hand. Waiters moved through the room carrying trays of hors d'oeuvres. The room quickly quieted down as Betty started with her typically bubbly, excited welcome speech. "Now, I know you have all heard about Lisa."

A spattering of boos swept through the room at the mention of Lisa's name. I looked around, trying to figure out what I was missing. Why were they booing? I happened to really like Lisa. She was an amazing trainer who had been part of the program from day one.

"I know. I know. I am just as angry as all of you. Now, Lisa really tricked us. She used us just to turn around and stab us in the back. She was disloyal and traitorous! She abused my kindness and generosity. She stole and corrupted our image." Betty shook her fist as she shouted to the crowd, who met her energy and then some. All around me, women were getting visibly angry, scowling and shaking their heads. I was worried someone would produce a pitchfork and light torches to storm the poor woman's house.

It turned out that Lisa had committed the cardinal NTR sin. She had been a top certified stylist and trainer at Betty's salon, one of Betty's right-hand women. She had brought in several other stylists who were trained, certified, and worked alongside her at her salon. Then, one day, without warning, she walked out on Betty, taking all of her stylists with her to start her own salon. The NTR community exploded with vitriol, anger, and mean-girl-style drama. I had no idea how I had avoided it before then, but I was glad that I had. The hot seat drama felt like more than enough on a weekly basis.

"I will tell you all right now, if you are a person like Lisa, this is not the place for you. NTR is a community of women who support each other. Who devote themselves to the NTR method and don't just take what they need and run. Lisa revealed herself as the snake she is, slithering around for our secrets just to betray us in the end!" Betty shouted. The word choice was interestingly evangelical in nature, and quite frankly, I wasn't sure what to make of it.

Sure, Lisa doing a complete one-eighty made me vaguely uncomfortable. Maybe she saw something I hadn't. But even if she abandoned ship for a good reason, was I willing to throw away my own career because of it? Not really.

Betty's speech set the tone for the entire convention. Everyone talked about Lisa's betrayal. Not a speech or presentation went by without targeted hate toward Lisa and her group of stylists. It was so powerful, so compelling, that I almost started to believe it was warranted. My logical brain reminded me that anyone could change paths or leave a company, while my emotional side nodded along at the betrayals, thinking I never wanted to get on Betty's bad side.

"Guess Lisa's betrayal is good news for Tiffany," a woman named Marissa leaned in and whispered in my ear.

"What do you mean?" I asked. I really felt out of the loop. All I knew about Tiffany was that her husband owed her $6,132.87. Why would Lisa being dragged through the dirt help her in any way?

"Tiffany turned on Betty too. From what I heard, she felt absolutely mortified after her hot seat and now she can't stand anything having to do with NTR," Marissa explained.

"That's nuts!"

"Yep, and if it wasn't for Lisa going AWOL, I'm sure Betty would be talking more about Tiffany. Apparently, Tiffany is so mad that she is posting all over her social media about how awful NTR is. And she's even found a new extension method."

I shook my head in disbelief. It seemed like a lot of drama that I wasn't really interested in being part of. At that first hot seat session, I thought Tiffany should focus her energy on her business, not what her husband owed her. Similarly, I thought Betty was spending too much time worrying about her "enemies."

But then, finally, Betty announced a piece of real news. News that made the Lisa drama irrelevant. Betty had developed a new, exclusive, licensed stylist program. She would accept only 250 women into the program, so only the best of the best would be allowed. It was exactly what I had been looking for—a way to grow and improve. The rejection of my shadowing request no longer mattered, so long as I had a path to move forward. The new program came with the added perk of being included in an NTR searchable database, so when potential clients were looking for a local stylist, my name would pop up as a licensed provider.

"In order to apply, please submit thirty threaded rows along with the application," Betty instructed at the close of the conference. That was all I needed to hear. As soon as the convention was over, I hopped a flight to New Orleans and got to work. There were other requirements, of course, but the selection process would be based mainly on the thirty rows, and I was determined to be first.

I locked myself away with a mannequin head for a week, beading row after row after row until my fingers went numb and I thought my brain might turn to mush. But I did it. I finished. I beaded the last row and sat back to breathe and admire my hard work.

The blood drained from my face. My mannequin was half bald.

I sat back with my hands clasped tightly over my gaping mouth. There was a straight, thick line across the scalp of the mannequin that contained not a single strand of hair. All around me, stray clumps of fallen hair lay scattered on the floor. I couldn't believe it. I stepped back, scrubbing my hands across my face to collect my thoughts. I paced the room a few times, stopping in front of the mannequin to be sure my eyes had not deceived me.

But there was no denying it. The NTR extensions had caused baldness. I looked closely at the mannequin head. The non-silicone beads had been breaking off several hairs every time I clamped them on. They were too rigid, and so they damaged the hair. What was worse, I knew that kind of friction might cause permanent damage to hair follicles.

My hands were clammy with sweat, and my heart raced. I was a fraud. All this time, I had been destroying my clients' hair. I stopped in my tracks, doing mental math. If every month I put two rows in the same place, and after thirty rows the clients would lose their hair, then they would start seeing bald spots in twelve to eighteen months. Betty's policy of turning over clients every eighteen months suddenly made a whole lot of sense.

My hands found my head, and I hurried to the bathroom. My assistant had been putting the same NTR extensions in my hair. Standing in front of the mirror, I ran my fingers through my hair, finding the extensions.

"Shit," I said. There, in the mirror, I saw that my hair was thinning. The start of a bald patch stretched across the back of my scalp. "Oh, my God! My clients!" I cried. My head started to spin, and I felt like I couldn't take a full breath to fill my lungs. I had to sit down. What the hell was I going to do? I had transitioned all of my long-term clients—clients I'd had twenty-plus years—to these hair extensions. I even told them that if they weren't doing color or extensions, I wouldn't be their stylist anymore. And all along, for about nine months, I had been damaging their hair. I couldn't in good conscience continue doing NTR, but I also couldn't just throw away my entire life's work. I loved extensions. I loved coloring. What the hell was I going to do? Start cutting men's hair? Give up on my passion? Turn away all of my clients? Any of those choices would absolutely ruin my career.

I sat in front of my bald mannequin and cried for a good thirty minutes before wiping the tears away. I had to do something. I had to find a new method. I suddenly remembered what Marissa told me at the convention: Tiffany had found a new method. I pulled up Instagram and searched for her. Marissa hadn't been kidding when she said Tiffany spent months shit-talking NTR. Her page was filled with posts about Betty specifically. None of them went into specifics about the NTR method, though. Possibly, Tiffany hadn't gotten far enough in the program to realize the inherent hair-loss problem.

I wondered if other women in the program knew the dirty little secret. Was that why Lisa had bailed too? It didn't matter, in the end. In that moment, I decided I wouldn't be silent about why I was leaving. It wasn't my job to keep Betty's secret. I felt betrayed. I felt swindled by Betty's bullshit. She and her husband had roped me in, and others like me, with their promises of seven figures, fool-proof marketing strategies, and an amazing method, only to lie and cheat, turning me into a fraud in the process. I couldn't stay silent.

No wonder Betty rejected my application to shadow her for a couple days. I would see right through her pyramid-scheme bullshit. She knew me well enough at that point to understand I wasn't one of her blind followers. I would see things as they were, and I wasn't afraid to push back. Her money didn't come from real clients. Her money didn't even come from teaching us the extension method. It came from stringing us along, over and over again, making us pay to play, month to month. NTR didn't care if I left, because they had duped ten other girls to take my place.

I knew I had to leave. The only question was, where would I go next? That was where Tiffany came in. Mixed in among her rage posts about Betty, she shared information about a new extension method. It sounded promising.

CHAPTER SEVEN

I walked back into Urban Elements the next morning to a full schedule of color and extension clients. I took a deep breath and got to work. The previous night, after wiping my tears and draining my wine, I signed up myself and two of my stylists for a conference in January hosted by JLM, the method Tiffany promoted on Instagram. JLM was an up-and-coming extensions method named after its developer, Jenna Lee Malory. I stepped into this one with a little more trepidation than the last, but not much. I wouldn't learn that I was susceptible to cult-like talking points until much later, after making many mistakes.

I was all too easily dazzled by the beautiful pictures and the largely empty promises. Every time someone stood on a big stage and said, "Look at everything I have. You can have it too!" a part of me shouted, "YES!" Their knowing, precise words tugged at the little threads that kept me up worrying all night. They fed into the image I had about where and what I should be by now. And all it took was one little tug until I was unraveling and reforming my business practices around their models of success. So, when I saw JLM on Tiffany's Instagram, I was ready to jump on board. I was leaving one sinking ship for another, but I couldn't see the water pooling at my feet.

JLM, unlike NTR, carried some amount of credibility because Jenna was a registered nurse. My logic was that since she was in the healthcare industry, then she had a better understanding of how to put in extensions without making people go bald. Logic, reasoning, and powerful emotional draw aside, I had no choice. I couldn't stay with NTR, and I couldn't turn my clients away either. So, there I was, walking into work, carrying the heavy burden of knowing I was a fraud while doing my client's extensions.

January couldn't come quickly enough. Each day of those couple of months felt harder than the last. Every time NTR came up on my Instagram feed, I oh-so-badly wanted to leave a comment, letting everyone know that the method makes clients go bald, but I resisted.

Part of me really wanted to bring them down. I wanted to watch them burn. I had spent upwards of fifty grand on their education, courses, and conferences—money I could have set on fire for all the good it had done me. But it was about more than the money; I was disillusioned. They made promises they knew from the very beginning they wouldn't be able to keep. Their entire system was a scam.

But the other part of me felt like I should keep my disappointment with NTR under wraps so my clients didn't run for the hills. Also, I didn't dare start a war with NTR that I had no hopes of winning. Betty had the ability to bring me down in a way that I may not be able to bounce back from. I watched it happen to Tiffany. They ended up suing her for slander, and because they had the time, money, and resources, it didn't go well for Tiffany.

In the end, NTR's success or failure didn't matter to me. I wanted to find a better method. I wanted to win and come out on top despite them. And I could acknowledge that I had learned a lot about business from them; I had no problem giving them credit where credit was due while working toward my next steps.

By the time January came, I felt like I had spent a lifetime applying extensions I didn't believe in and a lifetime fighting against an immovable force. I thought I would breathe more easily walking into the JLM conference, but it wasn't what I had been hoping for. I had signed up for the one-day, eight-hour educational program, so I already knew it was a far cry from the three-day conference that introduced me to NTR. Also, they hadn't sent any material ahead of time—no videos to watch, no packets to read; I was walking in blind to what the JLM method might entail. For all I knew, it was worse than NTR and I was wasting more time and money. So, I already have some misgivings.

When my two assistant stylists and I arrived at the venue, my worries were not eased. It was nowhere near the same caliber as NTR's conference. I had flown the three of us to Seattle, only to find a salon that looked like any other salon, situated in a strip mall between a convenience store and a Chipotle. It contained ten workstations, which gives you an idea of how big the space was—a bit smaller than my salon. The front area looked dated but well-maintained. Of course, as a salon owner myself, I found it all too easy to judge other people's spaces, so I tried to resist mentally criticizing the place. The receptionist checked us in and walked us to a large education space in the back, packed with thirty people. Practice dummy heads were mounted on tripods with three people per dummy head. I shared a look with my two stylists, but we stepped into the room and found an open tripod we could share.

When it was time to get started, there were no speeches, no big promises, no elaborate shows meant to pull us in. The three teachers simply got to work demonstrating the technique, and then walked around the room while we practiced. None of the teachers seemed a hundred percent sure of what was happening, who was leading, or how to run the seminar. Overall, my key takeaway was a sense of disorganization. The presenters talked over each other and stepped on each other's toes. I hated to keep comparing it to the NTR conference, because…well, as we now know, NTR is trash. They were selling a lie. Yet, the allure was real. They sold their brand as being more than a hair extension method. It was an entire way of living. They wanted their certified stylists to eat, sleep, breathe, live, and die by NTR. And everything in their presentation supported that idea.

When I let myself be honest about my initial impression, JLM felt like a huge step down, leaving me torn. I didn't want to like anything about NTR after feeling betrayed by them, but even in the midst of this new training, I missed them. I missed feeling like I was part of something exclusive, special, and really upscale. At least, thanks in large part to Tiffany and her mission to take down NTR, many heavy hitters who were at the NTR conference a few months prior had since left NTR and were at the JLM conference too. They were likely in the same situation I found myself in.

The JLM method itself was a mixed bag. They didn't use beads, which gave me instant relief. The chance of damaging the hair and scalp is way less without beads. Instead, they used a wrap method reminiscent of the friendship bracelets I made in elementary school. An initial knot was tied to the hair, and then the extension was wrapped into it. It worked. It didn't seem to damage the hair. But it was time consuming.

I left the conference eight hours later with sore fingers, aching feet, some disappointment, and a little bit of hope. I didn't need JLM to be flashy. I just needed a method that worked well. I could use the marketing strategies I had already learned from NTR (guess it wasn't all for nothing after all), and I could make it on my own. I already had a booming business at the salon. Of course, I wanted to go bigger. I wanted to expand my own education and the education I offered to others. And, if I was being honest with myself, I wanted a way out of the salon with Rylan.

Since the shocking revelation two Christmases prior, things had settled. Rylan kept up her end of the bargain and was no longer taking money out of the business to fund her personal life. But the entire experience left a sour taste in my mouth. I didn't want to share a salon with someone like her, nor was I all that interested in shelling out ten thousand a month just to open the door. More and more, I was learning new and better ways to manage myself as a brand, as a commodity. I wasn't sure I even needed a storefront. But I couldn't escape my lease for one more year since we had extended it when we expanded. My only choice in the meantime was to stay the course, look for more opportunities, and learn as much as I possibly could.

With my new certification, I dove into the JLM method. I methodically removed all traces of NTR from my Instagram and replaced it with JLM, although not without some hesitancy because it didn't take long before I started getting bad vibes from Jenna herself—surprise, surprise! She was like Betty in many ways, and yet also the direct opposite. Betty came from big money and was trying to further a lifestyle she was already used to (by collecting a following of stylists who would empty their pockets once a month). Jenna, on the hand, seemed to come from very little. Yes, she was a nurse, but that had zero influence over her brand, business, or method. Her involvement in extensions was more happenstance than anything else. She had discovered the method (likely co-opted it from a black woman who had been doing it her whole life) and started marketing it. The whole thing felt kind of gross. The success of any given method was timing, marketing, luck, and, of course, financial backing. JLM's success was due to showing up at the right time, as just enough people were turning away from NTR and looking for a new method.

JLM filled a need for me: I could keep my clients. But I wasn't entirely sold on the company like I had been with NTR. I plodded along, always looking for new opportunities. I had recently quit being a Davines educator after doing the math and realizing that I was spending more money being educated than I was educating, but I continued to educate on color theory and hair extensions. I continued to present at hair shows independently, showcasing my talent.

On my birthday in March 2019, I was doing a show in New Orleans when my phone rang; my mother's number displayed on the screen. My relationship with my mom had its ups and downs throughout my childhood and adulthood, but we had largely reconciled, and we checked in with each other every so often. I dismissed the call, assuming she wanted to wish me a happy birthday. When my phone vibrated again, concern began to worm its way through me. But I dismissed the call again, switched my phone to "do not disturb," took a deep breath, and refocused myself on the show.

At the end of the night, I pulled out my phone and saw several missed calls from my mom and brother. Real panic hit me. There was no way they wanted to wish me a happy birthday that badly. I dialed my mom's number with shaking hands.

"Mom? What's going on?" I asked.

"Rachel, I'm so sorry. Bubby died."

CHAPTER EIGHT

My entire world narrowed to the sound of my mother's voice, the violent beat of my heart, and the rasping of my breath. I couldn't fill my lungs, and it felt like the ground was spinning out from under me.

"No," I said.

"I'm sorry," was all she said.

I don't know what the rest of that conversation sounded like. By the time it was over, my cheeks were streaked with tears. I couldn't lose my grandmother. I simply couldn't. Through everything I had experienced, my Bubby—my grandmother on my mother's side—had been the one and often only constant in my life. When my father was struggling with a hidden drug addiction, she was there. When my parents were divorcing, she was there. When my mom worked all the time and I was practically raising my brother, she was there. When I was having my first daughter as a single mother, she was there.

When I went through my divorce, she was there. She was a stabilizing force through all the turmoil and doubt.

There was little resemblance between Bubby and me. I had an equal mix of my mom's and dad's features, which meant that I could pass as either black or white (with a tan), but Bubby was a little, old, white Jewish lady who absolutely adored me. In my teens, when my mother wasn't around, I had Bubby to teach me life lessons and guide me and just love me. Although, she was convinced that I should have married a Jewish man.

"Is she having an identity crisis?" she asked my mother one day.

"What are you talking about?" my mother asked.

"Did you know she is dating a black guy?" Bubby whispered conspiratorially. My mother and I just laughed.

"Mom, look at her. You think she is going to date some white guy with a yamaka?" she asked.

Bubby simply thought that Jewish people should marry other Jewish people. Even so, she did not let her belief affect the way she treated us. Both my daughter and stepson are darker than I am, and she loved them just the same. They were the light of her whole world.

It is funny the moments you remember while grieving. I tried to wipe away the stream of tears, but they just kept coming.

The next morning, I woke up to an onslaught of notifications on my phone. In my fog of grief and exhaustion, I tried to make sense of them. Most were some variations of "congratulations." The effusive positivity jarred uncomfortably with the utter despair I was in. I had expected condolences, but instead, I was getting excited, cheerful messages. I sat up, trying to figure out why the hell people were congratulating me at a time like this. As far as I knew, I hadn't done anything worth celebrating. I read through my text messages to no avail and then pulled up my Instagram feed. After thumbing down through several posts, I found it. Jenna had, unbeknownst to me, made me an educator with JLM.

In truth, being a JLM educator didn't mean much. I was already included on her Facebook list of providers; now I was also added to her list of educators and invited to a private Facebook group. It didn't change my day-to-day in any significant way. Still, I wrote blanket thank-yous to everyone who had reached out and made a quick post announcing the change myself before adding it to my profile. When I had finally finished the obligatory work-related tasks, I fell back onto the bed, phone lying on my chest, reality sinking in. Every time I let myself get distracted for a moment, my brain was immediately pulled back to my Bubby's death like it was brand new information.

I didn't know how to live in a world without her, so I didn't, as best I could anyway. I moved through the motions of grief, but I barely let myself feel them. The tears came later that night and over the next several days in heavy, body-shaking sobs, but then, I pulled it all back in as much as I could.

I had children to raise and a business to run. I put my head down and focused on putting one foot in front of the next, letting my routine carry me through each day.

Despite trying to distract myself, I couldn't help but notice how much my intuition had heightened. I felt a stronger connection to the unseen world. In some ways, it felt like Bubby wasn't really gone for me in the same way she may have been for others. I couldn't put my finger on why or how or exactly what I sensed, but I knew she was there. That feeling helped me get through each day.

The weeks passed in a whirlwind of grief, confusion, and hard work. I used my status as an educator as best I could, offering more training in the salon and traveling to other locations to teach the method. Unfortunately, I was still lukewarm about the JLM wrapping method. It was worlds better than the damaging NTR beads, but not as seamless as I felt it had the potential to be.

My business and my brand grew. I was getting better and better at marketing, gaining clients, educating, and managing the behind-the-scenes tasks of the salon, yet I couldn't shake a nagging feeling. I felt unsettled, like I should have been doing something, but I didn't know what. I felt my Bubby's presence often, urging me on in some unseen, unknown way that I couldn't possibly understand.

On May 14, on my daughter's birthday and two months almost to the day since my Bubby's passing, I woke up at three a.m., which was starting to become a pattern. There was no telling what exactly woke me up. It could have been a bad dream that I failed to remember or a stray stressful thought, but, either way, there I was, climbing quietly out of bed, grabbing my phone off the nightstand, and trudging blindly into the bathroom while my husband snored lightly from the bed.

The bathroom light blinded me momentarily, and I blinked several times, trying to adjust my eyes before sitting on the toilet. I scrolled through Instagram, registering little while my tired mind tried to catch up with my physical body being up and out of bed.

"Go to China. You're going to start a hair company." Bubby's voice reached my ears as if she were standing directly beside me.

I jolted and sat upright, startled, with a racing heart and wide-eyed panic. Any residual sleepiness fell away. I searched the small bathroom, knowing full well that I was absolutely alone. Yet, I had undeniably heard my Bubby's voice.

"Am I going crazy?" I whispered to no one.

"Go to China. Go to China." The words came two more times with a clarity and conviction that I had never heard before. I had experienced a general, vague sense of her presence in my life since her death, but never had I heard her voice, let alone such a clear and strange instruction.

What on earth did she even mean? Why would I go to China? What did China have to do with my salon or even a hair business like she suggested? I leaned back, letting the cold porcelain ground me to reality as I glanced down at my phone.

I almost never let Instagram stories play out on my feed; instead I constantly scrolled, looking for inspiration. But when I heard my Bubby's voice, I had abruptly stopped scrolling, and my feed landed on an ad that was replaying over and over. When my attention finally returned to my phone, my breath caught in my throat all over again.

Yandy Smith, the star of *Love and Hip Hop*, a reality show on VH1, was on my story feed announcing a May Vendor trip to China.

"Vendor trip to China! Find supplies to start any company you can imagine," she announced. I immediately thought about a problem I had been considering for a while: the difficulty of buying just one weft (what the industry calls small bundles of hair that become a single extension). I believed someone needed to create a solution that would make wefts more accessible.

I clicked on the story to get more information and saw that they were leaving in two weeks. I took a deep breath and filled out the form, right there and then, sitting on the toilet at three in the morning. When I get a sign from the universe, I don't tend to ignore it.

The next morning, after an anxious, restless night in bed, I woke as soon as Reco stirred.

"I booked a trip to China," were the first words out of my mouth. He looked at me with his calm demeanor and blinked the sleep out of his eyes, waiting patiently for me to continue. "I have to get hand-tied hair to start a hair company. You have to go with me."

He sighed. "Are you kidding, Rachel? How many more of these get-rich-quick schemes are we going to do?"

"This isn't a get-rich-quick scheme," I argued. "Neither were the other things I have done. I am trying to build a brand and a business."

He groaned and rolled over. "If you have to do this, then go ahead, but I'm not going to China."

"Fine," I said. I recognized it was an issue he wouldn't budge on, no matter how great the end reward may be. So, I hurried downstairs, put on a pot of coffee, and called Nica.

"Nica!" I practically shouted once she answered.

"Oh, boy, what now?" she asked. Over the years, she had gotten used to my antics.

"How do you know something is up?" I asked.

"You are never this perky before your morning coffee unless you have a new scheme."

"Fine. You know me too well. You have to come to China with me. I have to purchase hair," I said.

"Okay, I wasn't expecting that. Can you start from the beginning?" she asked. I could hear her sipping coffee, trying to wake herself up.

"Yandy Smith is organizing a vendor's trip to China. I want to get wefts to sell. We can start our own company. Right now, only one company, Olivia Nine Hair, sells quality hair for the hand-tied method. There is absolutely room in the market for a competitor. If we wait too long, we will miss this window," I said. I knew I was talking too fast, like I tended to do when I got really excited, but I felt an urgency moving me forward.

Nica was not from the salon, hair, or beauty world. From our time as friends, she had picked up on enough of the drama and inner workings to follow along, but she was business-minded, a practical balance to my more dreamy, impulsive nature. I just hoped I could convince her to jump in on my half-baked plan, because although I had put it together with short notice, I knew it could really be something.

"Maybe we should draw up a business plan and a market analysis," she said.

"There isn't time. The trip to China is in two weeks," I said. "Listen, I know it sounds crazy, but I just need you to trust me on this." The sigh on the other end of the phone meant I was winning her over. I couldn't stop a smile from creeping across my lips.

"You know that I have your back, but there is no way in hell I am going to China," she said.

"Oh, come on! I can't go alone!"

"You have to," she said. "I will be a partner in this business, but I can't go to China. So, you get the wefts, and I will work on the rest."

"You are the best!" I exclaimed, although a solo trip to China would test even my independent nature.

After dishing all the few details I had, I canceled my plans for the day and headed to San Francisco, where I filled out the paperwork for a rushed visa to China. I spent half the day waiting for bureaucrats to manage my information, get me forms, and review everything.

When I was finally done, my phone rang. I didn't recognize the number. Normally, I would let it go to voicemail, but, given that I had just signed up for a trip to China, which I still couldn't believe was real, I figured I should probably answer it.

"Rachel?" the unfamiliar voice said on the other end of the line.

"Yes?"

"Hi, this is Ayanea with the vendor trip to China."

"Oh, hi!" I said, excited.

"I just wanted to go over some details with you. When you filled out the form, it said you are looking for hand-tied hair?" She hesitated before pronouncing the last three words as if they were completely foreign to her.

"Yes, that's right," I said.

"And what is that?" she asked.

"A type of hair used in hand-tied hair extension methods."

"I see," she said, pausing. "Most of the women that join us on our vendor trips are looking for several types of things in a wide category of products. You are looking for only one very specific product. Unfortunately, I don't know if you will find that. I will have to make some calls. If none of our partners in China have hand-tied hair, we will have to cancel your trip."

"If you work with a hair factory, then you have access to hand-tied hair," I explained.

"We work with only one factory because they are the best. I will reach out to them and let you know," she said.

With that, my spirits plummeted. I was so sure that the vendor trip was the thing to do. I was so sure my Bubby had pointed me in that direction. How could the venture be over before it even started? I paid more than fifty-five hundred dollars on blind faith that the trip was the best and only choice to grow. I had been testing hair for Olivia Nine Hair to provide honest reviews of their binds in return for a small discount on their products. They were really the only hand-tied hair company on the scene. If you wanted quality hair, you had no choice but to use their products. I saw that as an opportunity. There was absolutely room and demand within the market for someone else to come on the scene, but that required quality products, which, in turn, required the trip to China.

"When will I know?" I asked.

"I don't know. I have to make some calls. I will get back to you in twenty-four hours," she said.

When I got off the phone, I didn't know what to do with myself. I was looking at the longest twenty-four hours—and perhaps the biggest letdown—of my life.

CHAPTER NINE

I checked my phone constantly, expecting that somehow, despite it never leaving my hand, I missed a call from Ayanea, the woman running the vendor trip. My business plan—as much as it was a plan—was only viable so long as I had product to sell. So, I moved through the next day completely distracted, doing my best to keep customers happy, wondering if I would have to clear my whole schedule in two weeks. Nica checked in every so often through texts filled with exclamation points and emojis. Each time my phone buzzed, a thrill of nervous anticipation shot through my veins before looking at my screen and checking for news on the trip. The day passed, followed by night, without the phone call I had been anticipating.

That night, I lay in bed willing myself to go to sleep. My husband snored gently beside me, the kids were fast asleep in their respective rooms, and I pondered Bubby's message. Had this not been what she meant when she spoke to me that night?

Was it just some half-dreamed, wishful thinking? It was easy in the bright light of daytime to keep moving forward, to ignore doubts and follow my new path with certainty. It was harder when I was alone with my thoughts in the darkness of night.

I believed that what I heard was a message from Bubby, but was I somehow misinterpreting it? Had my last two forays into the world of extensions been a waste of time? I was still an educator for JLM. I had found success by any measure. I was happy with that yet still not satisfied. JLM filled a need, but the cracks in Jenna's method and her poor overall management style had begun showing from day one. JLM didn't feel like my final landing, and neither did Urban Elements.

My eyes eventually grew heavy enough to pull me into sleep. I awoke with a startle as my phone buzzed on the bedside table. I sat up, heart pounding, as I fumbled to pick up and unlock my phone.

"Hello?" I said, trying to sound awake and somewhat professional. I hadn't even looked at the number.

"Rachel?" came the voice on the other end. It was Ayanea. I tried to decipher if her tone held good news or bad news, but there wasn't enough in that one word to go on.

"Yes," I said, climbing out of bed and padding softly down the stairs. My husband was already stirring, but I hoped he could fall back to sleep.

"I am sorry I didn't get back to you sooner, but we heard from our manufacturer in China." She paused, waiting for an acknowledgement of some kind.

"Oh, no problem," I said through gritted teeth. "What did they say?"

"They have hair." A wave of relief washed over me. Thank God! I was going to China. My mind raced as the woman went through the details of the factory and the trip. I did my best to listen and write down what I could. As soon as I hung up with her, I called to check on the status of my visa and was promised it would be ready.

The next week and a half went by like a dream, like I was living out someone else's life while waiting for my own to start. I packed all my necessities into one carry-on bag, packing as light as I had ever packed in my life. Then I put one empty suitcase inside another larger, empty suitcase, twice, giving me four empty suitcases to fill in China.

I climbed on board alongside many other hopeful entrepreneurs looking to start businesses. I had no idea if any of their plans, products they hoped to find, or business infrastructures were viable. I imagined that some of the people who settled in for the thirteen-hour flight would drop money on products that they simply couldn't sell. Others might have a real chance at an online business. I hoped I fell into the latter category. I trusted my gut and my vision. There was a market for high-quality hand-tied hair. I just had to tap into it, and with what I learned about marketing through NTR, with the connections I made in the extensions world, and with Nica's business sense, I thought I had a pretty good shot. That didn't stop me from spending the entire flight running what-if scenarios through my head, round and round.

Eventually, the white noise of the plane lulled me to sleep, and I woke up as the jet made its final descent into Guangzhou. I climbed off the plane and was careful to stay with my group. Every sign was in Chinese, as I had expected, but the airport was surprisingly crowded. There was no escaping the push of people that threatened to sweep me away like a riptide in the ocean. Outside the airport, it was no better.

We found our hotel and then quickly moved along to the factory. It was about what I had expected. Instead of letting us inside the actual factory, they took us to a hot, dimly lit warehouse full of products. When we got there, the other people in our group spread out, searching the tables for hidden, unique treasures that would populate their online stores and make the trip worthwhile. I, however, knew exactly what I was looking for. I made a beeline to the table set up just for me. As soon as I touched the hair, I knew it was high quality. I put in an order for twenty-five thousand dollars' worth on the spot, although I didn't exactly have a plan for how I would get that money; but like everything else, I trusted all the pieces would fall into place. Then, I filled my suitcases with hundreds of dollars' worth of beads, clips, grippers, and looping tools I could package and sell with the wefts. The beads I bought were silicone-lined to protect the hair, instead of damaging it like the NTR beads did.

With full suitcases, I re-boarded the plane back for the states. My worry had dissipated significantly since seeing the hair. It was better than I could have imagined. If I played my cards right and lined up my marketing strategy, then the whole thing would take off like wildfire.

When I got home, I FaceTimed Nica. She was anxiously waiting to hear what I found.

"They're perfect!" I said. "They're exactly what I was looking for."

"I knew they would be. I had Sarah go ahead and get started on the website. When will the hair ship?" she asked.

Sarah had been a good friend of mine since my early days out on my own, working in high-volume salons. We had bonded in high school over drugs and parties. When I got sober before my daughter was born, we didn't see each other much, although we loosely stayed in touch. When she was on drugs, I understandably had a hard time being around her. But she got clean and became a web designer, so when I needed help, I reached out. It was like no time had passed. She jumped wholeheartedly into Everything Hand Tied—the name I had settled on for my new business.

"They need a couple of weeks," I said.

"Good. That gives us time to get the e-commerce platform ready," she said, and once again, I was so thankful to have Nica on my side. "So, how are we covering the initial shipment of hair?"

"I have one idea. We need an investor," I said. Nica just raised her eyebrows. She knew whatever I had in mind was probably not the traditional way people went about getting investors, but she trusted me.

When we finished talking, my eyelids were so heavy, I could barely make it upstairs to my bed, despite it being only late morning. The normal exhaustion after a quick trip was compounded by the time change. I dragged myself to bed and slept for half the day.

"How was China?" Reco asked when I finally emerged, just in time for dinner. I made my way around the table to give each of my kids a hug and kiss on the head before finding my spot at the table. I looked at the spread of takeout Chinese food, which looked nothing like the food I had eaten from its country of origin.

"Interesting," I said.

"Did you find what you were looking for?" he asked.

"I think so," I said, a smile spreading across my lips through the fog of jet lag. His question was a simple and straightforward one. He was asking if I had found the hair. But I was answering the question on a deeper level.

I had been searching my whole life for an identity and place that felt like a good fit. After working for other salons for years, I opened my own salon, thinking I could create a culture that reflected me in a place that was all my own, so whenever I walked in each morning, I would feel at home. A place where I would be unconditionally accepted, and no one would tell me I didn't belong. Instead, I ended up with a partner who wasn't much better than the women who had run me out of every other salon I had ever worked at. Then I found the NTR extensions. I thought that was the right fit. I loved learning and helping and educating, only to find out that I was destroying people's hair, the one thing I was meant to be improving. I had moved to the less damaging JLM method, but I wasn't enthusiastic about it or the company behind it. Now, on the brink of this latest project, I could honestly answer that, yes, I had found what I was looking for. I didn't think it was my ultimate stop, but it was an avenue in which I could explore what I had to offer and who I was as a leader. I needed to get my new venture up and running. But first, I had to get the investor I had in mind on board.

The phone rang only once before a familiar voice picked up. "Hey, Rachel," Jo said on the other end of the line.

"Joanne, let me take you out to dinner tomorrow night. I have a business proposition for you."

Joanne had been coming to Urban Elements since I opened it. Most clients came in every three months to move their existing extensions and every six months for replacements. But Joanne came in once a month, like clockwork, and got brand new extensions each time. It cost big money. She couldn't have been over twenty-five; maybe she was even younger. I never asked what she did for a living. I guessed she was a sex worker, but I never pried. I just knew that she showed up with five thousand in cash every four weeks.

The next night, I found myself sitting across from Jo. Her style was Bohemian chic, like you might see at an exclusive music festival. I could only guess that her dress, strappy sandals, long beaded necklaces, bracelets, and rings cost more than most people make in a year or two.

"Can I start you ladies off with a drink?" the waiter asked. He wore a nicely fitted suit in keeping with the upscale quality of the restaurant.

"I'll take a Cosmo," she said. I smirked, wondering if she had recently watched *Sex and the City*, where Carrie Bradshaw turned cosmopolitans into a girls'-night-out classic, although the original run of the show was before Jo's time.

"I'll have a Merlot," I said.

Jo smiled sweetly as the waiter walked away then turned her attention to me. "Well, spill it. What's the business proposition?" she asked with a devious smirk.

I smiled. "Listen, you don't have to disclose any of your private life to me, but you obviously do something that affords you a pretty nice lifestyle and makes you a good amount of money."

She nodded.

"I want you to go into business with me. I don't have the financial capital, the cash, but you do. I am starting a hair company with high-quality hair for extensions. I will do your hair once a month, free of charge, if you will help me get this company up and running," I said.

"How much?" she asked.

"Twenty-five thousand," I said, eyeing her for signs of hesitation, but she just shrugged nonchalantly.

"Sure."

We spent the rest of the meal talking a little business and a lot of gossip. The next day, she showed up in the salon with a paper Chipotle bag of cash. It was the strangest business transaction of my life. I had to stuff it in my purse and leave it there for the rest of the day until I could get to the bank.

"I got it!" I shouted as Nica walked into my house at the end of the day.

"Do I even want to know where from?" she asked, as she dropped her things by the door like she lived there.

"Probably not," I said. She shook her head.

"Here. Let me show you the website," she said. She typed in the URL and brought it up. My breath caught in my throat. There it was. In big, bold, white letters on a clean black background were the words: Everything Hand Tied. I sighed and blinked back tears. It was real. I was really doing it. I was creating something from nothing.

I nodded, not trusting my voice. "Looks good," I managed when I finally composed myself.

"I'm proud of you, Rach," Nica said, rubbing a hand across my back. I nodded again with a smile. It felt better than I had expected. I had found success in so many ways up to that point, but somehow seeing my webpage felt different. It felt really good, like I had made something special. I was ready to throw my hat in the ring and see where it would take me.

But nothing could have prepared me for the backbreaking, finger-splitting work of prepping all the hair I had ordered.

CHAPTER TEN

The hair arrived in giant crates. When I lifted a lid, I found weft upon weft nestled in protective plastic packaging. I may have had a website, but I didn't have any sort of automated system to turn the wefts into professional looking products. The whole point was to make high-quality extensions. There was no other way to do it than to get my hands dirty; I was going to have to manually brand, label, and ship each order of wefts along with a tin of beads for attaching the wefts to hair. I hung my head at the overwhelming project before me. Then I sent a group text to everyone who had agreed to be part of my new venture, attaching a photo of the bins:

Who's up for a packaging party tomorrow?

The next day, I sat cross-legged on my living room floor, surrounded by my business team. To my great relief, they had all responded right away and showed up at my door in the morning, ready to work. From the get-go, the team included Joanna, who was, to my great surprise, on board with showing up and helping behind the scenes in addition to being a financial backer; Reco, who, after his initial hesitation around the trip to China, went all-in on my business; Sarah, my old friend and web designer; and, of course, Nica.

We started by putting the beads into twenty-gram packages. I felt a little like a drug dealer as I weighed the tiny beads and slid them into tins. We did a lot more work in the next few months: cutting and gluing hair to make our own color rings, designing and producing our own packaging, managing marketing and social media, taking orders, carefully checking each order to make sure it included everything the client wanted, putting an Everything Hand Tied sticker on each order, boxing the orders, writing the shipping labels by hand, and shipping the product. It never ended. We were truly a mom-and-pop, arts-and-crafts operation. There wasn't a single step in the process from beginning to end that I wasn't personally involved in.

From the get-go, I didn't leave anything up to chance. I had gathered many connections in my early days as a Davines educator, in all the salons I'd worked in, in my own salon, and in the world of extensions. I knew people, and I made it a point to reach out to every single one of them as soon as the hair from China was in my possession. I invited old clients, students, and salon owners out to dinner. I bought expensive bottles of wine and, sometime during the course of those meals, I'd pull out a sample of the product I was offering.

It didn't take much to sell Everything Hand Tied. For the most part, the quality of the hair spoke for itself, so all I had to do was promise a personalized feeling unlike big, faceless companies, and most people hopped on board. Any doubts I may have had while sleepily weighing beads at night subsided as orders started coming in.

Those orders were a light at the end of the tunnel, while at the same time they created more exhausting, endless work nights. I worked at the salon all day, just to come home to fulfill orders, weigh beads, print invoices and packing slips, inventory product, and balance our budget.

But we grew. With that growth came the money to automate some tasks. Of course, we still had to weigh the damn beads, but we were moving in the right direction. Within a short period of time, my little at-home, hair-project pipe dream had turned into a real, bona fide business with processes, employees, and professional packaging. It felt pretty good, and not just because I was no longer working eighteen-hour days developing blisters on my fingertips.

The success of Everything Hand Tied only worked to highlight how unhappy I was with JLM. I found myself longing for the structure and organization of NTR. Every time I caught myself thinking fondly of my time at NTR, I shook my head forcefully, trying to dislodge such ridiculous thoughts. I didn't have a choice but to stay the course. I couldn't leave JLM. For one, I didn't have a replacement method for applying extensions. Two, I wanted to participate in the Extension Expo Conventions Jenna was hosting in September.

Admittedly, she had a cool idea for a convention. Her goal was to bring together as many different extension methods, stylists, and vendors willing to participate as possible. The event was designed to create a sense of community in an often drama-fraught group of people. Every method swore the other methods were copying them, the stylists had beefs against each other, and the vendors were in constant competition. There was very little cohesion, camaraderie, or sharing. That meant isolation and less innovation. Jenna's philosophy was that the market had enough space for all the methods. So, when she announced the Extensions Expo Convention, I thought, "Huh, that's a good idea," for the first time since joining JLM.

What really sealed the deal for me was Jenna's offer of an Everything Hand Tied booth at the convention, where I could market and sell my extensions. Normally, vendors paid for booths because of the opportunity to get in front of thousands of potential clients and customers. But, since I was both a JLM stylist and educator, she offered me a booth for free. That was huge. So, I was stuck with JLM for at least a couple more months, which was fine, since I was so busy focusing on Everything Hand Tied.

A few months in, I got a call from our lawyer. We brought him on to manage all the legal, behind-the-scenes nonsense that happens in all businesses large enough to draw attention from competitors or gripes from customers looking to benefit in some way.

"Rachel?" he said when I answered.

"What's up, Mark?" I asked. His tone had me worried.

"I wish this was a pleasant call, but I think you have to remove Joanne from Everything Hand Tied."

"What? Why?"

"I just think it would be dangerous to be associated with the kind of work she does. You are opening yourself up to all kinds of lawsuits," he cautioned.

"Wait, you lost me. Why is it dangerous?" I heard a heavy sigh come through the other end of the line. "Just tell me."

"That original twenty-five thousand that she contributed to the business came from her sex work. She is a madame. You don't want your company associated with Heidi Fleiss type of money, do you?" he said.

"Oh, shit," I muttered.

"You need to buy her out," he said. I nodded on the other end of the line, even though he couldn't see me.

Joanne was a good friend. I felt terrible even approaching her with any of that. She, and her money, had been there when I needed a financial backer. I also had no judgement for how she and anyone else found their way in this world. But Mark was right. I had to distance the business from her money. Sometimes, I found myself wondering if she was really all-in anyway. She helped with customer service and other miscellaneous tasks that came up, but she often made little mistakes. I found myself wondering if she would be happy with a buyout to focus on her other business.

Approaching her was easier than I thought. "Listen, I just talked to our lawyer," I began.

She must have read reluctance, regret, or pity in my voice because before I could even continue, she said, "It's okay, Rachel, just say it."

"He thinks the way you make your money might look bad for the business. He thinks I should buy you out."

"Oh, that's all? That's fine," she assured me. And that was that. Since she owned twenty percent of the company, it was easy math to cut her a check based on what the business was worth. In only two months' time, she made thirty thousand in profit—not bad. Her attitude about the buyout reminded me, again, just how lucky I had been throughout my life to find a group of truly amazing, supportive people.

With that settled, I prepped my product for the Extensions Expo. It would be the first showing of Everything Hand Tied, and Jenna was promising three thousand attendees, so it was a big deal. I bought tickets to fly the entire team to Phoenix, Arizona, with strict instructions not to pack anything in their large suitcases. All of their necessities had to fit into their carry-on bags because I needed their suitcases for product.

In the days leading up to the flight, we carefully packed wefts, beads, and tools into the suitcases. I wanted to be able to hand over whatever people purchased on the spot rather than taking orders and shipping purchases later. At the airport, we checked our bags and boarded the flight with tempered excitement.

When we landed in Phoenix, I was first hit by the overwhelming dry heat, and I questioned how anyone could live there. As we drove through the endless deserts with plateaus reaching for the startlingly purple sky, I understood.

While the landscape may have been breathtaking, the conference center was quite the opposite. It was a large room in a low-end hotel chain found on the side of every airport highway. There was little signage and not a single living soul to direct us where to go.

We found our booth after walking the perimeter of the entire conference room. It was loud and chaotic. Nobody seemed to be in charge of a single thing. The vendors were doing their best to set up their booths and direct people to their spots. Once the doors opened, the attendees shuffled through without a real sense of where to go or what to do. I kept an eye out for Jenna. I got a few glimpses of her here and there, but she was largely absent.

At the end of the night, I sighed and shook my head. The three thousand attendees we were promised never showed; in fact, less than a thousand people attended. The event was just another glaring example of Jenna's shitty management style and even shittier planning and marketing skills. She clearly hadn't spent any energy getting the word out about the conference. We packed up our stuff and left feeling extremely frustrated. I made *some* profit after factoring in expenses, but only because I didn't have to pay for the booth.

That experience cemented my decision to leave JLM. I had to find an alternative extension method as soon as possible, though I didn't yet know what it would be. The next day, I logged onto the JLM Facebook page out of curiosity to see what people were saying about the conference. And that's where I found my answer.

CHAPTER ELEVEN

The private Facebook page dedicated to JLM educators was a chaotic mess in the same way the entire program had been. In mid-September, Jenna posted that she was rolling out a new method called the Hidden Method 2.0 for reasons I didn't fully understand. Possibly, she just wanted to drum up more interest in her method or to stay relevant. Or maybe she really had developed a better method. (To be clear, when I say *developed*, I mean "borrowed" from other stylists who didn't have the means to promote their methods on their own.) Regardless, as I scrolled through the posts, I saw a lot of people talking about the 2.0 method. I also saw ladies asking questions, complaining about clients, and spilling tea relevant only to themselves. There was so much drama that it was hard to sort through, especially since I wasn't sure what I was looking for. To understand a single post, I had to scroll back through months of other posts and hundreds of comments to find the beginning of the story, which wasn't worth my time.

Even so, I stuck with it, hoping to find some relevant piece of information that might guide me toward something new. That's when I read the latest piece of angry, scandalous gossip, filled with JLM try-hards clutching their pearls at the horror of it all. One woman, whom I didn't know because JLM hadn't created enough of a community for me to know more than a handful of girls, posted a screenshot of a Hidden Row Hair (HRH) ad. HRH was a company in Utah, brand new on the scene. They had been running ads that looked a lot like organic posts. The ad in question showed a method that shared similarities to JLM's 2.0 method. The text above the image said, "Look at this woman who stole from JLM!!!!!" The post had accrued twenty-five comments and counting, all expressing outrage. A couple months before, when I still wore my JLM blinders, I might have agreed with them. But by then, I was suspicious about JLM in general and the post specifically. Something didn't seem right.

I had seen the same ad about a week prior to the Extensions Expo, filed it away to look into later, and hadn't yet gotten around to researching it. Countless extension startups were looking to push out the top names in the industry and create brands for themselves, making it hard to separate authentic, high-quality companies from scams—although, in retrospect, they may have all been scams in their own right, but that's a story for another book.

I jumped over to Instagram and found the original HRH post/ad. I saw they had launched on September 1, two weeks before Jenna introduced Hidden Method 2.0; there was no way they had stolen JLM's 2.0 techniques. I sighed and rolled my eyes. So much drama. Sometimes, I wondered how all these ladies had so much time and energy for the endless gossip. But while I was there, I scrolled through HRH's offerings. I liked what I saw. Their ability to organize and market far outpaced JLM. The website looked professional, organized, and eye-catching. Most importantly, they had a formal process for becoming a member of their team. The first step was submitting an application; the next step, an interview. They successfully presented themselves as a high-end alternative to other poorly put together, shoddily managed methods.

In hindsight, it is hard to say if the method, delivery, and imagery was all that much better than JLM's or if I was simply desperate for a new experience; but I decided, without much planning, to make the move. I studied the page with stars in my eyes. HRH offered exactly what I had been so desperately craving: a status symbol, methodology, and education system all wrapped into one, with the bonus of being very green, so they'd probably appreciate some direction and had lots of opportunity for growth. Before I knew it, a wide smile stretched across my lips. "Thank God," I whispered as I ravenously consumed every blog post, every Instagram image, every tidbit of information available. I felt like I had been starving and was finally given a proper meal.

Yet, I didn't immediately fill out the application. It asked for social media handles, so I first examined my Instagram profile with a critical eye. I tried to view it through the lens of those deciding whether to recruit me into a new, exclusive, high-end method. What would they see? Did I fit their aesthetics? My obvious affiliations with JLM had to go. If recruiters from HRH saw on my profile that I was a JLM educator, they would delete my application immediately. I clicked edit, then hesitated, my fingers hovering over the keyboard.

Every hair extension method has devoted followers who don't look kindly upon all the other methods. People outside the industry would find it hard to believe just how cutthroat and exclusive the world of extensions can be. A typical customer shows up to a salon, asks for extensions, sits in the chair, and pays for the service without ever knowing the careful calculations, tense negotiations, manipulations, in-fighting, and blind devotion that went into the stylist choosing, learning, and using the extension application method.

I tried my best to stay above it all, but if I wanted to learn the HRH method, which I did, then I had to play the game a little bit. If I left my JLM affiliation on my socials, HRH would see me as an enemy. They would assume that I was trying to learn their method just to bring it back to Jenna or to undermine them in some way. Plus, they would probably think poorly of me if they knew I was with JLM. I had gotten the sense in the previous months that stylists not working with Jenna looked down their noses at JLM's methods. Jenna's chaotic leadership and lower-class reputation preceded her and tainted her educators' reputations.

I hesitated before deleting JLM from my profile because I wasn't officially quitting them yet. If I scrubbed all evidence that I was a JLM educator, I wondered what Jenna might say. Would that be enough to prematurely end my relationship with them? Then I pictured Jenna taking the time to look through my Instagram and laughed out loud. She would never. She probably never once bothered to look at my socials. There was a distinct possibility that she made me an educator without even knowing who I was. Her business strategy had always been impersonal. She believed the bigger the better, even if it meant using lower quality resources.

I shrugged my shoulders and deleted JLM educator from my bio and removed all posts and tags that mentioned it. When I was done, I realized it didn't matter much to me. I had already decided my time with JLM was coming to an end, anyway. I would keep using Jenna's method until HRH accepted me (since, again, I had to keep providing extensions to my customers), but I didn't have any strong loyalty to Jenna herself. Unlike NTR, whose presentation and promises enraptured me at the start, JLM had always been simply a means to an end.

I felt a strong pull toward HRH, similar to the pull I'd experienced with NTR. I just knew they would be the answer to all my problems. I would finally find my people. They were nothing like JLM or NTR. They were sleek and high-end but also personal and caring. They were small and brand new. I imagined being able to get in there and get what I needed from them yet remain above the drama inherent in such a company.

I was already sold on HRH from their general forward-facing presentation, but when I saw their "flip up" (any hairstyle that pulls the hair upward, like a ponytail, bun, or elaborate pile of curls on top of the head) on Instagram, I nearly gasped with excitement. I get it; it sounds dramatic. But the flip up is the greatest downfall for salons that offer hair extensions. That's because flip ups have a high potential of revealing the beads or glue used to attach extensions into the natural hair. Other "no show" methods promised minimal appearance of beads, but often missed the mark, making it impractical for women to wear their hair up. But when HRH said no show, they meant no show. I studied the pictures and videos of hair pulled into high ponytails and flipped and tossed, and I never spotted a single bead. I had to know how they did it.

Despite my strong pull toward HRH, I hedged my bets and signed up for two other up-and-coming companies that didn't require applications. I ended the night feeling good. I had an application in to HRH and the opportunity to learn two other methods. I felt in control, something I sensed a lot of stylists offering extensions were looking for. The need for control over their lives and finances often entrapped them in predatory programs, but not me. Not anymore. Not after my experience with NTR.

Or so I thought at the time. I was too innocent and starry-eyed as I imagined my new life with HRH to recognize the familiar tactics of an insidious, manipulative organization with the ability to sink its claws into me and derail everything I had worked for.

CHAPTER TWELVE

Within the week, I received an email requesting a phone interview with Ron Taylor from HRH. He introduced himself as Abby's husband. Abby was the woman behind the HRH method. From the second I got on the phone with Ron, I could tell he was one of those people who are naturally easy to talk to. He was charming, personable, and interested in what I had to say.

"Good morning, Rachel," he said. "I'm glad that you reached out to HRH. It looks like you know a few other methods. How did you first start out in extensions?"

I was so glad that he didn't start with the dreaded "tell me about yourself" request. I never knew how to answer that. It's not that I had trouble talking about myself. In fact, that was part of the problem. If you ask me to tell you about myself, I might end up giving you my whole life story! So, it helped that Ron's questions were more specific right off the bat. Without getting into too much of the drama around my salon or why

I left NTR, I explained my passion for educating, my love of extensions and hair from a young age, and my desire to grow myself as a brand. From there, the conversation shifted from interview to dialogue. I felt like I was talking to someone I had known for longer than fifteen minutes.

Just like Christopher from NTR, Ron seemed to know exactly what I needed to hear. Interestingly, what I needed to hear from Christopher in October 2017, while trying to keep my salon afloat after Rylan almost brought me down, was very different from what I needed to hear in October 2019. I no longer needed someone to fill my head with glossy, idealized visions of success. I didn't need to be reassured that my dreams could come true. And I didn't need anyone to step in and tell me how to market myself to the world. I had all those things already. What I needed at that time was a community of like-minded people. I needed an organization I could help mold and build and create as a way of expressing myself, and that was what Ron was offering.

Everything Ron said felt like it had been scripted exclusively for his conversation with me, and while I knew well enough to understand that wasn't true, I still felt like I had found my place. We talked about my twenty years' experiences as a hairdresser, my time with Davines, and the various extension methods I had learned. I talked about how important education was to me and how I used the space in Urban Elements to bring in as many opportunities for learning as I could. I even mentioned Everything Hand Tied. From my end, I saw any collaboration with HRH as an opportunity to grow my weft side business by being associated with the newest, hottest trend. Ron likely saw an opportunity to collaborate with a successful hair seller to bolster the validity of his company.

During our hour-long call, Ron described how he and Abby started HRH, just the two of them aside from a few contract photographers and models. He said they were building the business from the ground up because they believed so wholeheartedly in the method they were trying to share. He confessed to some of the challenges they faced, along with their successes. He also shared just how vitally important it was to them that HRH be accessible. They didn't want their method to be out of reach or too exclusive for anyone.

Something about that last line of thinking dug deep into my psyche and hit a nerve. For my entire career, I had been looking for my place, looking for some affirmation that I belonged, that I was welcome. Each place I landed left me more alone than the last; I was always on the outside looking in. The idea that a method existed to welcome everyone made my heart just a little bit lighter.

His admissions conveyed a sense of vulnerability and trust. If I had any doubts leading up to my interview, that one conversation assuaged them all. I wanted in on the ground floor. I wanted to learn from Abby, but I also wanted to act as a guiding influence for her, too. From what I could tell, HRH didn't have an education or mentor program to speak of. They were unseasoned and inexperienced, and I had a lot of valuable insight to share.

The next week, I got an email announcing my acceptance along with links to videos. Their entire training program consisted of online videos sent in three stages. They offered no conferences, no in-person meetings, no one-on-one or even group sessions to demonstrate the method. I immediately started making a mental list of how I might improve both the onboarding and the online education.

I remembered the feeling of showing up at NTR's conference at the Ritz on the California coast feeling like hot shit. I had been so thoroughly taken in by the smoke and mirrors of it all. The allure of the lifestyle clouded my better judgement of who the people behind the method were. I didn't think that HRH needed anything like that. In fact, I was glad they were more low-key. I also didn't think they needed a JLM-style conference: thirty bodies crammed into a sweaty back room taking turns working on mannequins for hours at a time. But there was certainly room to grow beyond the series of online videos they provided, and I planned to be the person to help them do so.

I dove into the videos, carefully watching and rewatching as I practiced on my own mannequin head. The courses were a learn-at-your-own-pace kind of deal, and of course, I was determined to finish them at breakneck speed. When I decided to do something, I was all in, no hesitation. I envisioned spending ten or more years with HRH until I was ready to retire. The sooner I became certified, the sooner my future could start. So, I watched the videos and submitted my work via WhatsApp directly to Abby. She sent feedback on what to improve or redo, and I quickly followed her directions and re-submitted. I was a quick learner. I had been doing extensions for a long time, and despite the newness of the method, the basics were the same. Once Abby approved all my work from the first videos, she sent me the next stage of videos.

I blew through all three stages in about thirty days. When I sent my last submission, I received confirmation of my certi-fication. I immediately updated my socials and website. Abby added me to a registry of HRH-certified providers, which I was really excited about. The idea of an extension stylist data-base was brand new and, frankly, I was surprised that no one had thought of it before. Creating a searchable list of all the certified providers in any given area seemed a genius way to help customers find stylists.

I breathed a sigh of relief at being certified. Even though it had taken only a month, it felt like such a long time coming. I had so many ideas floating around in my head on how I would market myself, grow my salon, and work with Abby to become a mentor, educator, and, hopefully, even more.

The first step, of course, was to get my girls at Urban Elements certified in the method. No one even close to lo-cal was performing the HRH method, so the more certified stylists at my salon, the more attention the salon would get. I helped my stylists apply and interview, and they all got accept-ed and received their training videos.

Once my stylists finished the do-it-yourself courses, I sat down in the stylist chair and asked them to work on my hair for practice. I was just as desperate as anyone else who regularly wore extensions to have the latest and greatest, and I liked the bonus of being able to put up my hair with ease. Also, wearing what I was trying to sell was important so that when new clients debated about what kind of extensions to get, I could lift up my own hair and show off the hidden beads.

Only a few minutes in, I knew that something was wrong. I felt like tiny needles were pricking my scalp, as if my head was on fire.

"This shouldn't hurt that much," I said, pulling away. My red-flag radar blared inside my head. I had visions of the bald patches created by NTR. My heart sank. I had dumped so much time and money into the HRH method already; even worse, I had hung such high hopes on my new life with HRH. If they turned out to be just another scam, I would be so devastated that I wasn't sure how I would pick up the pieces again.

I took a deep breath and steadied myself. I couldn't write off the method after one brief, bad experience. Perhaps my girls just weren't doing it right. They had learned from a video, after all. Once I composed myself, I pulled up Abby's Instagram and sent her a DM:

Are you still taking new clients?

CHAPTER THIRTEEN

I waited anxiously for a response. Luckily, I didn't have to wait long. Abby messaged me back with a simple "yes," a yellow thumbs-up, and a smiley face. I couldn't help but laugh. Interpreting emojis from someone new always presents a challenge. Did her emojis mean she was excited? Did she include them out of habit? Who knew? But I was one step closer to understanding the person behind the new method that I had tied myself to.

I replied: *I would love for you to do my hair and get to feel this method on my own head.*

She wrote back: *Yay!! Let's get you scheduled!*

We planned for a time that I could fly to Utah. A lot was riding on this one appointment. I needed to know HRH was the real deal and not just another scam. I had to make sure Abby was not just another rich woman attempting a money grab at my and every client's expense.

As well-traveled as I had become over the years, I hadn't spent a lot of time in Utah, which, interestingly enough, was a hotbed for extensions and extension companies. I don't know what I had been expecting from the Mormon capital of the world, but Abby's neighborhood certainly wasn't it. The Uber drove through winding, sprawling streets filled with giant McMansions built on acres of property. The neighborhood had a Stepford-wife vibe; even though each house had a unique lay-out and style, there was something unimaginative about them that I couldn't quite put my finger on. I expected all the women to come outside wearing 1950s dresses with tight bodices, flared skirts, and frilly aprons. But I didn't see a single soul—not a kid playing, not a lawn being mowed, not even a pet lounging out-side. That was more unnerving than anything else.

The Uber stopped in front of a sprawling house with Mexican-tiled roof and stucco siding, like something you'd see on a tropical vacation. I thanked the driver and stepped onto the driveway. I gazed at the three-bay garage, double front doors, and elegant veranda. On the left side of the driveway was a smaller building that could have been a rental property, guest house, or office. I stood in indecision as to which door to knock on until Abby stepped out of the small house.

"Hey there!" she shouted. She rushed down the three porch steps and embraced me in a hug. "I'm so glad you could make it." Her smile was blinding and genuine. "Come in, come in," she said, ushering me into the small building, which turned out to be her posh, well-decorated, upscale, one-chair salon.

I found her unabashed wealth so interesting. It was a far cry from where I had come from, but it didn't exactly represent the kind of success I wanted. I didn't find myself envious or enamored, like I had been at NTR's fancy convention. Instead, I was just curious.

"So, what does your husband do?" I asked. I thought I might meet him, but so far, he was absent from our appointment.

"Oh, he works full time for HRH now. Before that he created some software that did pretty well. We get a kickback every time someone buys it, so that's pretty nice," she answered.

I nodded. It was nice to have a passive income flow. It must have been what bought them the impressive house across the driveway and the opportunity to take the risk on the kind of business venture that HRH presented. Extensions are a fairly profitable business if you play your cards right, but I had seen countless ventures fizzle and burn before they even got off the ground. A successful extension business requires the perfect combination of marketing, funding, quality, and luck.

After a little small talk, Abby motioned for me to sit in the stylist chair. "Let's get started," she said.

I sat, anxious to finally learn what I had come to learn. She started working on my head, and I watched carefully in the mirror. I waited for the familiar burning sensation that I felt when my girls were putting in the extensions, but it never came. Abby worked quickly with delicate fingers. I felt her movements as she picked, combed, and divided hair before pulling it into a bead, but it felt no different from any other experience at any other salon.

I took a deep breath of relief. The method was the real deal. I didn't have to cut my losses and run. HRH proved to have safe, comfortable, invisible, and beautiful extensions. It almost felt too good to be true. I imagined that somewhere, just out of sight, a caveat lurked in the background, but the longer I talked to Abby, the more comfortable I felt.

She was clearly just as green as I had expected. She had been a stylist for only three years, which, in the beauty world, is considered brand new. The company, for all its flashy images, consisted of only her and her husband working tirelessly to market, interview, send onboarding videos, and review submissions. As I listened to her, I knew that she could use my help just as much as I could use her method.

A grin spread across my face. We were a perfect match, and I had no doubt we would make a great team as I helped her grow her business. Perhaps that was my first mistake, giving myself to someone else's vision. Of course, I didn't know it was a mistake at the time.

"What about mentors?" I asked when she had finished complaining about how much work she was doing.

"Mentors?" she asked. She had to know what mentors were, but clearly, she hadn't thought about how mentors could help take some of the burden off her shoulders.

"I can help you!" I said excitedly. "Listen, you have done such a great job marketing HRH that it has become the most sought-after method out there. You have to be ready for massive growth and the influx of more stylists than you will know what to do with."

I could tell by her expression reflected in the mirror that she was seriously considering my words. It amazed me that she hadn't considered the exponential growth of her business. She seemed both savvy and naïve at the same time. She understood the potential of her method but hadn't put plans in place for growth. That gap in her business plan was a great inroad for me. I saw myself becoming a sort of mentor to her as well as to new stylists. I had been in the business for twenty-plus years at that point. I knew how things worked.

By the time I got out of her chair, I was excited about all the future possibilities. I also felt like I was walking away with a new friend. Like me, she seemed like an open book. We talked about kids. Although she didn't have any yet, she wanted some soon. We talked about husbands and childhood and beauty—about anything that came to mind. She was easy to talk to, and I imagine she felt the same about me because there was never an awkward pause or struggle to figure out what to say next. Our conversation was seamless and full of energy and emotion. It was a refreshing change from my relationship with the last two company owners I had been involved with.

At both NTR and JLM, the owners tried to create a façade of friendly, down-to-earth, intimate connections with their stylists, but they failed miserably. They had both gotten carried away with their own images and cult of personality until they were far from relatable. They created the illusion of being a part of something while keeping me and everyone else who joined them at arm's length. Conversely, Abby embraced closeness with her stylists. She welcomed meeting me and hearing my ideas. More than that, she was relatable. I felt like I knew her and really understood her. I understood what she was trying to build, and I was all for it.

At the end of the appointment, she hugged me in the driveway as I waited for the Uber to take me back to my hotel. I spent the night in Utah before boarding a plane the next morning. It was an exhausting whirlwind of a trip, but well worth it. I left feeling rejuvenated and excited that I could confidently tell my stylists we were on the right track. I could show them how to perform the method without causing pain, and we could start marketing ourselves.

The high of success lasted only so long after stepping back into the real world. Don't get me wrong—things were good, for the most part. Everything Hand Tied had taken off, steadily growing as more and more stylists found their way to the high-quality product we were selling. But Urban Elements was another issue altogether. No matter what I did, I could never get out from under the crushing debt that the salon seemed to carry. My stylist chair was always full, as were the chairs of the other stylists there, and yet paying the bills was still an overwhelming burden. I strongly suspected that Rylan was still mismanaging money, and I still carried a lingering resentment over her stealing from the business. I found myself frequently ruminating: Who does that? Who steals from her own business? There is no reasonable end game except maybe bankruptcy, in which case, there would be no more money to fund her fancy sweater habit.

I had no choice but to continue trying to run the salon, at least until the lease was up in another year. At that point, I would have to decide what to do. Would I close the doors and just chalk it up as a loss? I pushed the thought out of my head. I didn't have any answers yet. It was all I could do to keep showing up every day, to keep my salon business running, fulfill orders for my side business, take clients, market myself, and continue my education. And soon I would have to add mentoring to my to-do list. Making life-altering decisions about the future of the salon felt like a step too far for my exhausted, overworked mind.

I worked twelve to sixteen hours a day to keep all my plates spinning; I was constantly running and juggling. In some respects, it was a labor of love, but in other respects, I felt like I didn't have a choice, and I would have gladly let one of the plates fall.

It was December 2019. Little did I know that in a few short months everything was about to change, in more ways than one.

CHAPTER FOURTEEN

"One more year. Just one more year," I whispered to Izzy as I set up my station on January 2, 2020. Izzy smiled and winked. She knew what I had finally decided: when the salon's lease was up, I was going to leave.

"You can do it, girl," she said with a nod of her head. The bell over the door jangled, and Rylan walked in with a chunky knit rainbow sweater, Venti iced latte, and brand-new acrylics. I took a breath to keep my face under control and stop the eye roll that threatened to escape. In fairness, Rylan had kept up her end of the bargain. She had stopped stealing from the salon. But she did nothing more than that. She made no effort to market the salon, pay down our debt, or further her education.

My goal was to pay the bills, keep the doors open, and make an escape plan. When the lease ended in a year, I would bail without a single regret. The question of what I would do next felt like an open door leading to possibilities. I planned to spend 2020 building Everything Hand Tied, growing with HRH, and finding a new space to open a salon. Izzy and Lacey were my co-conspirators. They knew every detail about Rylan's betrayal. They knew the doors to Urban Elements would close as soon as the lease ended. They were also the only two stylists I planned to take with me to my new salon, not because the other girls were unkind or bad stylists or even because they were Team Rylan. I just wanted a fresh start with people who understood my vision and had my back. I wasn't close to the other stylists, so it felt better to let them go their own ways.

A few weeks after flying to Utah to meet with Abby, I got a call. It wasn't entirely unexpected, but it was exciting, nonetheless. The call was the necessary first step toward building my relationship with Abby and my new brand as an HRH girl.

"We want you to be a mentor!" Abby said with an excited squeal in her voice. I smiled on the other end of the line even though she couldn't see me. "Rachel? What do you think?"

"Yes! Of course!" I squealed back.

Even just a few short months into their new venture, HRH and its method were blowing up, as I knew they would. Like me, every stylist worth their spot in a salon was always looking for the best extensions for their clients. Abby's no-show method really was revolutionary, but she simply didn't have the infrastructure to manage the influx of interested stylists. As a mentor, I took over part of Abby's responsibilities. When new stylists were approved for the HRH video course, they received training videos through email as before, and then they would learn, practice, and submit their work via videos. But now I, rather than Abby, was the one to review their work, give feedback, and approve them to move on if and when they were ready.

Within the first week, I had ten videos to critique. I watched the videos and either gave the stylists my stamp of approval to access the next portion of the course or sent them specific feedback on their techniques. I also answered any questions they had. Basically, I was their point person in the program. The next week, I received videos from ten more new stylists, then ten more, and it continued on until March, when everything changed.

The warnings about a mysterious virus started in February. News out of China reached the US as confused Americans watched, nervously speculating. It was impossible to discern whether viral videos of men in full biohazard gear walking the empty streets of Wuhan were real or fake. Even if they were real, did we actually have to worry? Mostly, we felt safe in our little first-world bubble. Surely, nothing too dangerous would ever reach us. People cracked jokes while secretly wondering if they should be stocking up on groceries.

Then, on March 15, 2020, the announcement came. The US was shutting down for two weeks to stop the spread of COVID-19, originally referred to as the Coronavirus. Businesses would close, people would stay home, schools would become virtual. With a collective nationwide gasp, we all wondered what the hell this would mean for us. I had no choice but to shutter Urban Elements' doors. In that moment, dread threatened to overcome me. How would I pay my bills for the month if I missed two full weeks of clients? But there was nothing to be done, so we put our worry aside and treated the two weeks like an unexpected vacation. The kids were home, my husband was home, and the whole world was on pause.

As the two weeks came to an end and we realized the shutdown would continue indefinitely, I started seriously worrying about my bills, the salon, and my hair business. I didn't have long to consider those burdens, however, because mentoring took off without warning. I went from having ten new mentees a week to close to a hundred. People were bored, sitting at home alone, wondering how to fill their time, and stylists, or hopeful stylists, decided learning a new extension method was exactly what they needed. Overnight, I went from spending an hour a day watching and commenting on videos to four or five hours a day. Mentoring threatened to take over every waking hour, including the time I dedicated to Everything Hand Tied, which, amazingly, hadn't yet been affected by the pandemic. (We didn't get shipments from China for six weeks, but luckily, I had enough hair stored up to meet demand.)

California continued to enforce a strict policy banning the operation of all "non-essential" businesses, but I didn't want to give up working behind the chair indefinitely as the government stumbled around trying to figure things out. While I could spend hours a day critiquing videos, that wouldn't be an option forever. I decided it wasn't an option at all.

The first decision I made was to hang dark, light-blocking shades on all the windows in Urban Elements and quietly open up to clients.

The next decision I made was to entirely revamp how I managed my mentees. After several months of working with new HRH stylists, I realized that they all had the same set of questions, experienced the same confusion, and needed the same guidance, with only slight variation. I saw an opportunity in that repetition. Rather than getting on individual Zoom calls or sending tailor-made responses, I started recording videos that addressed the most common issues. Every time I encountered a unique inquiry or issue, I made a new video to keep in my growing library of pre-recorded problem-solving tutorials. With my new approach, I managed to get my workload down from eight hours a day in front of a computer to only a couple of hours in the morning and a couple of hours at night.

A huge weight lifted off my shoulders. I had time to continue pursuing my own personal ventures: seeing clients on the down-low, sending videos to mentees, and taking orders for Everything Hand Tied. With those problems solved, at least temporarily, I was left to face the question of Urban Elements. Since closing the doors on March 15 and then secretly reopening, an idea had been forming.

As soon as the pandemic hit, I decided not to pay my rent. The government had quite literally demanded that my salon, as a non-essential business, shut down, but I was still expected to pay for rent and utilities? Nonsense. I tried my best to negotiate with the property owners, but they held firm. And so did I.

"Screw waiting a year," I said to Izzy. "We gotta cut our losses and get out now. We should start looking for a space to open a new cooperative salon."

Izzy looked at me with wide-eyed wonder. "You think so?" she asked.

"Yeah, I do. I am going to get out of this lease, buy Rylan out of the business, and then we will be free to do whatever we want." The more I talked about it out loud, the more excited I became. Izzy was nodding along, reflecting my own enthusiasm. Maybe I was too naïve, too excited, or too distracted to see anything beyond Izzy's seemingly genuine excitement. Or maybe she was just that good of an actress.

I spent a couple of minutes every day searching for a space and eagerly anticipating my next steps. In the meantime, I heard from the leasing company. They expected payments, so I got a lawyer and planned to fight. I wouldn't pay for a space I couldn't use. It was time to be done with everything that wasn't serving my larger, long-term goals and to cut my losses—that meant the salon, and that meant Rylan.

It would have been easy to simply walk away, to let the salon die right alongside the lease. But that would mean the name Urban Elements, with all the credibility it carried, would be lost too. Urban Elements as an entity had ten years of loan history and business success that would afford me a certain amount of clout when it came to banks and future loans. That was an intangible advantage that I wasn't willing to give up. The problem was that, technically, Rylan and I owned the salon and the name equally.

"Rylan," I said, broaching the subject over the phone. "I think it's time to talk about the plan for Urban Elements."

"Ummm, alright," she said. She was distracted and flippant, like she didn't care one way or the other.

"I'd like to keep the business," I said.

"Wait, what? I thought we were getting out of the lease."

"We are, but I want to keep the name and rights to the business. I'd like to buy you out."

"Yeah, sure, I don't care," she replied.

"Alright, I am working on paying down all the debt, and then we can talk about the buyout," I said. Something about that whole interaction felt suspicious. Maybe I was getting better at picking up on the drama that lurked just out of sight within the salon world, or maybe I was just naturally suspicious of Rylan. I sat with our conversation for a while.

I had just gotten the first communication from the leasing company's lawyer, and it was filled with a lot of legal language claiming the leaser's right to be paid rent regardless of the pandemic or the government's mandate. My lawyer was in the process of drafting a response and working on a motion to bring the issue to court, if it came to that. He wasn't optimistic about it being resolved any time soon. I was in a truly sour mood when I picked up my phone and texted Lacey:

You know what's up with Rylan?

I wasn't even a hundred percent sure I knew what I was asking. Something was always up with Rylan. She manufactured drama like it was her full-time job. But a few minutes later, my phone rang.

"Rachel," Lacey said when I answered, and I knew immediately from her tone that she didn't have anything good to say.

"What did you find out?" I asked.

"They already rented a space."

"Who are they?"

"Rylan, Izzy, some of the other girls." My heart sank at Izzy's name.

Once again, my bleeding heart had gotten the better of me. I spent so much time worrying about the well-being of other people that I naively worried that my two closest stylists would have no place to go. I told them everything because I wanted to make sure they were taken care of when I left. Now Izzy, along with several other stylists, were stabbing me in the back, and for what? I quickly got off the phone with Lacey to process the news, but all I wanted to do was rage at Rylan or Izzy or both. Instead, I texted Abby what was happening. Shortly after, my phone rang yet again.

"I heard you've been busy," Ron said on the other end. I hoped he had good news. Abby had likely told him about all the drama with the girls. I didn't speak with Ron quite as often as I spoke with Abby, but he made a point of keeping up and checking in periodically.

"I'm certainly trying. Times are crazy," I said.

"It's insane out there," he agreed. "I'm calling because I want to touch base about some thoughts I've had." The statement was just vague enough to leave me wondering if he had good thoughts or bad thoughts.

"Sure, what's up?" I asked, my whole body tense.

"I think there is a real opportunity with HRH and Everything Hand Tied," he said. I could have laughed. All my stress-induced adrenaline dissipated in a sudden rush. I don't know what I had been expecting Ron to say, but after the year I had, it could have been anything.

"Oh," I said, trying to change mental gears. "What were you thinking?"

"Obviously, HRH is doing really well, thanks in no small part, of course, to yourself and our other mentors. We are reaching a huge number of stylists and salons and clients. I think it would make sense to have a weft provider to go along with our method," he said.

I nearly gasped. Hearing his words made me a little light-headed at the possibility. He was right; HRH was becoming huge. Their method was spreading like wildfire through the stylist community, and clients all over the country were clamoring for HRH-certified stylists in their areas. I wasn't surprised. The method was amazing, and Abby and Ron's PR was on point. If Everything Hand Tied partnered with HRH to become the official weft of the entire method…I could hardly wrap my head around it.

I had done a pretty good job building Everything Had Tied through cold calls, by reaching out to everyone I knew in the industry, by attending conferences, and through massive social media campaigns. But it was hard work—hard work that had paid off in the end, but hard work, nonetheless. If Everything Hand Tied was branded with HRH, the growth would be exponential.

"I think that would be amazing. A partnership could benefit both of us," I said, and that was the truth. While it would be huge for my business, HRH would profit as well. Every time someone signed up for their program and bought my wefts, they would get a kick-back. Also, offering wefts to accompany their method would entice more stylists to buy package deals. I saw only good things in a partnership between us.

"Let's make it happen," he said, and I could hear his smile over the phone.

"Absolutely! I am on board," I responded. "I have so many plans for Everything Hand Tied. I want to be huge."

I thought back to when I first joined HRH. I had fantasies that joining such a new company during the early days would eventually give me a say and influence in the company, and here it was playing out to be true. Ron and I spent the next couple of hours on the phone as I detailed my ten-year plan for marketing and growth. I imagined how quickly joining forces with HRH would take me further than I thought possible.

I still had to confront Rylan, but at least I had something to look forward to.

CHAPTER FIFTEEN

"When were you going to tell me?" I practically shouted into the phone.

"Tell you what?" Rylan asked, even though she knew exactly what I was talking about.

"That you and the other girls got a salon?"

"I didn't think it mattered," she said, smugly. "We both knew that Urban Elements was coming to an end. How is it my fault that you didn't make plans sooner?"

Maybe she was right. Maybe I shouldn't have been mad at her at all, but instead at Izzy. But her actions were just another example in a long list of examples in which Rylan didn't think of anyone but herself, in which she didn't follow the norms of social kindness and decency.

"I understand that over the last ten years, we have had our ups and downs and professional struggles, but it seems really shitty that you would go behind my back and do this," I said.

"We didn't exactly go behind your back," she retorted.

"What are you talking about? If it wasn't behind my back, then what was it?"

"I don't know."

"Is this why you don't care if I buy Urban Elements?" I asked.

"Yeah, I guess so," she said. "We already have our new salon up and running. I'd like to get out of the other salon as soon as possible." I shook my head, at a loss for words. Technically, we still had eight months left in our lease, but with the pandemic shutdown, it seemed like the best time to try to sever ties.

"Alright, I'll let you know what happens with it," I said. When I hung up the phone, I sat in silence for several minutes. The betrayal from Rylan was nothing new, but Izzy had been a friend—a real, genuine, go-to sort of friend—as recently as the day before. Why the hell didn't she tell me that she was going in with Rylan? And why was she doing it at all? She had heard my stories. She understood exactly who Rylan was as a stylist, business partner, and owner. I assumed everyone else knew who Rylan was, too.

I called Lacey back. "I just don't get it," I said. Part of me did get it, of course. It was like every other salon I had ever worked at. The other stylists felt threatened by me and, as a result, created narratives to turn me into the bad guy. But in this instance, I was surprised. There was a mountain of evidence against Rylan, while all I did was encourage and support the other stylists.

"I heard that Rylan told everyone you were stealing money from the salon, not her," Lacey said.

"Are you fucking kidding me?" I stood up and started pacing around my bedroom, not sure what to do with the anger coursing through me.

"They also think that you were the one who spread the news about Bridget," she said. I could tell by her tone of voice that she was hesitant to share that little tidbit, knowing it might send me over the deep end. She wasn't wrong. The unfortunate culture of every salon I had ever been a part of was very similar to high-school, mean-girl drama. Stylists entertained themselves with other people's misfortunes and gossip, all while vying for the top spot in the popularity hierarchy. I wish I knew why that particular dynamic was so pervasive. I desperately wanted to prevent it at my next studio. Maybe I needed to be far more selective in whom I allowed to rent a chair. Although, no matter how careful I was, some people are just too good at pretending; Izzy was the perfect example.

Bridget had been one of my stylists. She decided she wanted to try her hand at acting, so she sent a bunch of tapes to various agents. The one who seemed interested turned out to be a scammer. She wasted a bunch of money, and I think she felt embarrassed about being fooled. She told me what happened in confidence, which I respected. I didn't say a word until I heard some other stylists discussing it while I got my nails done at the salon one day. I asked how they heard about it, and they turned in near perfect unison to gape at me with varying degrees of embarrassment and annoyance, I guess from being caught gossiping about someone else's misfortune and getting called out about it.

"Why are you listening to our conversation?" Izzy asked with a sharp tone to her voice that, in any other setting, wouldn't be anywhere close to appropriate. I wasn't exactly their boss, but I was the owner of the salon, which should have afforded me a modicum of respect. Although, as usual in the hair world, that didn't seem to mean shit.

"I'm not eavesdropping!" Right away I recognized defending myself was the wrong tactic. "If it was a private conversation, then you shouldn't have been discussing it in a public space."

"It wouldn't be a problem if you weren't listening," Izzy said.

"So, where did you hear about Bridget?" I asked again, this time ignoring her accusation.

"I don't think it is appropriate to say anything," Izzy replied, turning away from me and effectively ending the conversation. It was a strange exchange, but nothing too out of the ordinary for the salon. I didn't think much about it again.

Now I was finding out from Lacey that Izzy left the conversation that day and announced to Bridget that I was telling anyone who would listen about her failed and tragic attempt at becoming an actress. I think it was Izzy's effort to head off any accusations that I may level at her. Bridget, of course, joined their little collective coup. The smear campaign against me succeeded through small, measured assaults on my reputation, whispered from ear to ear until the majority of the stylists thought it best to take their chances with Rylan than with me, the devil herself.

I cried for a while. The whole situation was petty and stupid but also hurtful and lonely. When I first opened the doors to Urban Elements, I felt simultaneously that I had found my purpose and that all my dreams were coming true. I envisioned a space of community and learning. A space that would fill the gaping hole in my soul, the hole created by the drive to prove myself as a stylist, entrepreneur, and visionary.

Now, with the pandemic causing businesses to shutter, the debt piling up, and the ladies turning on me, Urban Elements seemed to be taking its last gasping breath in its current iteration. When your work is such a huge part of your identity, what does it mean when that work comes to an end? Did it mean I was a failure? Did it mean that I had somehow miscalculated? It was nearly impossible to not spiral out of control into self-doubt. I wasn't sad about Urban Elements closing. I just felt a sense of defeat in that chapter of my life. In that moment, I was incredibly thankful for HRH and Everything Hand Tied. I was indebted, really. They both gave me something to focus on while my salon imploded. I knew I had to look for a new salon space—eventually. But first, I had to get out of the legal knots the current space had me tied up in.

The fight to get out of my lease at the salon lasted nine months, from March to November. By that time, businesses had started to reopen. Rylan had opened her new space with the girls she convinced to go with her, although interestingly, Bridget didn't last more than a few months there. I didn't know if I should take some small satisfaction from that or just feel sad that the petty BS of salons struck again.

I put Rylan and her team out of my mind. I wanted to find a new space, but this time, I wanted it to be perfect, so I wasn't going to rush into buying or renting the first failing salon I could find, like Rylan and Izzy had done. Many businesses couldn't withstand the loss of revenue during the pandemic, so many spaces were available. It would be easy to swoop in, pay a fraction of what the space was worth, and start renting out chairs and doing hair. But I had a very specific vision for my own space. This time, I really did want to fulfill my dreams of a multifaceted space with chairs, an education space, a reiki space, and offices for Everything Hand Tied. I also wanted to bring in a group of doctors and nurses to do Ketamine treatments, weight loss medication, hormonal balancing, fillers, BOTOX, and IV therapy. I wanted an extra room that I could use to rotate short-term presentations. I wanted my new salon to be a one-stop shop for all my clients' health and beauty needs.

My days consisted of a 5:30 a.m. wake-up, an inordinate amount of coffee, a few hours reviewing work and questions from my mentees and sending out the relevant stock videos, several more hours managing orders for Everything Hand Tied, and then a few more hours of responding to mentees. I also combed re-al-estate listings, visited potential spaces, and talked to my lawyer about the ongoing case. I missed being behind the chair, but there was nothing I could do about it until I had a space. All in all, I had carved out a decent routine that left me mostly fulfilled while also moving forward toward bigger and better things.

"Babe," Abby said when I answered the phone one day. We talked at least once a week since the world fell apart in March and her business simultaneously took off. Sometimes we just chatted like friends, while other times we talked business. For the most part, Abby and Ron were great at marketing, but they didn't always know how to manage the mentees or the countless stylists signing up for their program, so they often turned to me for advice.

"What's up?" I asked. Her tone hinted at a serious, business-related conversation, so I prepared to listen.

"Some of the other mentees have reached out to me asking about you." I furrowed my brow. It sounded dangerously like the start of drama. I said nothing and let her continue. "You know, most of the new clients ask for you by name." She paused here as if waiting for me to explain.

It wasn't a secret that I worked my ass off to market myself on social media and personal outreach. My results spoke for themselves. I got girls certified fast through my attentive mentoring and quick responses. I had nothing to explain or defend about that. If the other mentors were talking shit, they were jealous, as cliché as that sounded. I felt my self-protective wall going up as my mind spun on the worst-case scenarios, as it all too often did.

"The other girls just don't understand how you are so responsive. They are spending so much time behind the computer trying to manage a fraction of the clients that you are. What are you doing differently? If I could get the other girls to be even half as efficient as you, then we could up our clientele countless times over."

I felt my body relax, releasing the tension I didn't know I had been holding. No one was bitching about me or making up new bullshit for a change. Abby was just looking for advice.

"I made stock videos," I said.

"Stock videos?" I could hear the confusion in her voice.

"Yeah," I said. "Everyone was asking me the same questions over and over again, so I made videos to answer them. That way I can just read their emailed questions and send them videos instead of being on Zoom all day long."

Abby was silent for a second. "That is genius!" she said, startling me. "Do you mind if I tell the other girls about it? Better yet, maybe I should make a whole bunch of stock videos. What a great idea."

The rest of the conversation was brief, and I could tell she wasn't really listening to anything else I said. Her mind was already racing, and no doubt she wanted to run the idea by her husband and start planning to scale up my idea.

"For the time being, could the other girls use your stock videos?" she asked right before getting off the phone. I felt put on the spot.

"Sure," I said hesitantly. I supposed it made sense to share my videos. Abby and I were on the same team. Our goal was to take HRH as far as we could, to build it as big as it would grow. To make it the name in extension methods. Still, agreeing to her request gave me pause. I had done a lot of work recording a complete library of videos. But I couldn't think of a reason not to share them. It only made sense. Like Abby said, if the other mentors could be more efficient, then HRH could triple or quadruple their business.

And anyway, whatever happened with the stock videos almost didn't matter; I already had my next move lined up.

CHAPTER SIXTEEN

My videos were circulating among the other mentors and being sent to answer their mentees' questions in what felt like a matter of seconds. It didn't matter, or at least that's what I kept telling myself. I had already put in the time to make them, and if sharing them grew HRH, then that could only be a positive. Still, it kind of felt like being the only one in a group project who was prepared on presentation day. Maybe it was enough that all the mentees saw my face instead of their mentors'. Like most things, I had to release my negative feelings about it, but a thank you would have been nice. Without appreciation, I felt, once again, like people were taking advantage of me. I didn't blame Abby. She was hustling, trying to get her business to grow, and I believed I was her right-hand gal, part of the team. But I expected something from the other girls—an email, a text, a phone call, *something*...

I was doing it again. I was letting myself get dragged into the high-school-like hair stylist drama. I took a deep breath and turned my attention to the suitcase that lay open and empty on my bed. I would be gone for only two days and one night, so I didn't need much, but I needed something. I rifled through my closet and pulled out a comfortable outfit for the plane and two nicer outfits to change into. In the stylist world, making an impression is important. I imagined that my image both online and in person was at least part of the reason that people hired me. Of course, the reputation I had cultivated didn't hurt either.

"Alright," I said as I came down the steps, carry-on in hand. It was the first time I would be at the airport since the COVID closures. Maybe I should have been nervous, but all I felt was excitement. I was excited to be out in the world again. I was excited to get my hands on hair and meet people face-to-face. "You have everything under control here?" I asked my husband. We both traveled a lot pre-shutdown, so we were both used to managing the kids, the household, and Everything Hand Tied solo.

"We'll be fine here," he said, leaning down to give me a kiss. I said my goodbyes to the kids, pulled up my mask, and hopped into the waiting Uber. I had seen news headlines about streets without the usual traffic and airports that had become ghost towns, but I didn't truly understand until I saw it for myself. We flew down the highway without the driver needing to tap the brakes once. At the airport, I got through security faster than I thought humanly possible. I wanted things to go back to normal, of course, but…a girl sure could get used to limited crowds.

I landed at Dallas Fort Worth International airport and stepped outside into the dry Texas heat where an Uber waited to bring me to my hotel. The next morning, I knocked on Cheryl's front door. I had never met Cheryl, one of my mentees, and we had spoken only a handful of times on the phone. But when she answered the door, she wrapped her arms around me, ecstatic that I was there.

"I am so glad you are here. This has been making me nuts!" she said. "I am just so worried that I won't ever get this right and then all that money will be down the drain." She spoke with a charming southern accent.

"You'll get it right," I said. She showed me into her house where her young kids watched *Peppa Pig* in the living room. In a spare-bedroom-turned-DIY-studio was a mannequin head and a phone set up on a tripod, ready to film.

She hadn't been the first of my mentees to complain about how hard it was to learn the HRH method virtually, to say she needed someone to walk her through the steps in person. But she was the first, of hopefully many, that I would visit to shadow. I understood my mentees' struggles. I wasn't the type of person to learn well through a computer screen, either. Whenever I tried, I found myself rewinding and pausing over and over again, only to be left worrying that I still wasn't doing it right. I was a stylist; I learned best by getting my hands on hair and watching techniques done in person. A lot of my mentees felt the same way. Even personalized videos that corrected their techniques or showed them different ways to do things just weren't enough to cross the barrier created by the screen.

So, when Cheryl had practically begged me with tears in her eyes to come teach her, I had agreed on an impulse. If giving hands-on instruction worked out and turned out to be something I wanted to continue, then I would have to run it by Abby, but I wanted to have proof of its success before I approached her. I had no doubt about how popular such a service would be, though.

I spent the day shadowing Cheryl. She showed me what she had been doing, and I walked her through the technique over and over again. I corrected her mistakes and watched her while she filmed the final test. By the end of the day, Cheryl was like a different person. Her nervous energy had been replaced by a light, happy confidence.

When I got back to my hotel, I found myself smiling. I realized I had needed this just as much as Cheryl had. I needed to be out among people. I needed to be teaching and helping my mentees in real, meaningful ways. The nagging worries about the salon drama and sharing my training videos and even finding a new salon seemed much smaller when I was busy making a real difference to people. I called Abby right away.

"Hey, babe," she answered.

"Hey!" I said.

"You sound happy," she observed. I laughed. I guess my good mood was more evident than I realized.

"I am. You'll never guess what I did!"

"What?" she asked eagerly, my own excitement rubbing off on her.

"I flew to Texas to shadow one of my mentees in person," I said. My stomach did little somersaults as I waited for her response. If she quashed the idea, then that was the end of my shadowing. As much as I felt like we were a team, she still had the ultimate say.

"Wow! How did that happen?" she asked.

"A lot of the mentees have been asking, and I decided to do a test run. I charged five hundred dollars for the day plus travel expenses," I explained. In truth, I wasn't sure if five hundred made sense or not. I had kind of pulled the number out of thin air. But it felt like as good a number as any to start with.

"And how did it go?" she asked.

"It was amazing. I think it was really valuable to Cheryl, and I loved getting out and about again. Do you think it's something I could offer to my other mentees who are interested?" Once again, I found myself anxiously awaiting a response. There was silence on the other end of the line. I could picture Abby's face scrunched up in thought.

"I think it sounds pretty good," she eventually said. I breathed out a sigh of relief. "I don't see any problem with it."

As soon as we got off the phone, I announced on social media and through an email blast that I was available to shadow mentees. The response was immediate and nearly overwhelming. HRH stylists who had never even mentioned being interested in in-person help were reaching out. I spent the rest of the evening responding to emails and working out a travel schedule that would take me all over the US. To say I was excited is a massive understatement.

Before I even landed back home, my calendar was booked for months. Of course, I left some time to continue managing Everything Hand Tied, looking for a new space, and mentoring my other clients, but I was traveling nearly every week. My heart was full. I felt amazing. My relationship with Abby and HRH was turning out to be better than I had originally anticipated, which was saying a lot because I had already had so much hope for it.

Months into my shadowing program, I got a phone call from Ron.

"Rachel," he said with his usual charm. "How are you? I hear you have been busy."

I had been busy. I had been shadowing mentees and building Everything Hand Tied, and I had even found a potential space for my new salon and Everything Hand Tied headquarters. The space was large enough to house a salon, offices, and a warehouse. The only downside was that it was largely unfinished and would have to be gutted and renovated. I worried it would become a money pit as we dumped more and more resources into it to create the exact, upscale salon I was envisioning. I had no interest in doing what Rylan had done—move from one prefab salon to the next, trying to work within someone else's vision. The space we were considering was perfect because it would allow me to let my imagination run wild in designing it; but, as my husband liked to remind me, we had to consider the cost. So, we hadn't made an offer yet, but I had a feeling we were close.

I didn't say all of that to Ron, though. He and I got along really well. I felt practically like a member of his family, but there was something in his tone, underneath the normal pleasantries, that made me want to get to the point of his call. So, I simply responded, "Yah, I have been busy."

"That's always good," he said. "Abby mentioned that you have been shadowing your mentees."

"Yes! It has been amazing. So many of the girls have been struggling to learn through videos. It has been so great to help them in person," I said.

"It sounds like it. Shadowing is something that I had been thinking about bringing into the program." His tone didn't change at all, but his words gave me pause. "Tell me about how you have been structuring it."

Incorporating shadowing into the official HRH program would mean a lot of things, and I didn't know if any of them were good. If HRH put structured systems in place for shadowing, clients wouldn't be able to reach out to me directly to get on my schedule. And, undoubtedly, HRH would set a price for the service and take a cut.

I couldn't help but wonder if Ron really had been considering this before I came up with and ran with the idea. I trusted both Abby and Ron, but I was business savvy enough to understand their desire to seize upon a growth opportunity when they saw one. I wished they had enough faith in me to let me continue to work independently. It was my idea, my mentees, my marketing, and my time that had made my shadowing program successful. I didn't love the idea of someone else stepping in and taking over.

Nonetheless, I explained to Ron how I was running my program. I went into great detail in the hope that he would keep the official program as close to mine as possible.

"That's great!" he said when I finished. "Listen, let's hold off on the shadowing for the time being until we get this system in place. I think having a uniform way of doing things would be best for you and the clients. Let's touch base soon."

"Can I finish up the clients who have already booked with me?" I asked.

"Sure," he said without much thought.

Relieved and cautiously optimistic, I hung up the phone. Surely Abby and Ron would do the right thing.

CHAPTER SEVENTEEN

"It's perfect," I said, spinning around the wide-open space to take in another full view of the facility we'd been debating about leasing. I couldn't keep the wide grin off my face. My enthusiasm was met with silence, and it wasn't until I stopped that I saw the skeptical expression—what you might even say was a scowl—on Reco's face. "What?" I asked.

We stood in the center of the huge, unfinished space that could best be described as a warehouse. In a previous life, it had been partitioned into an assortment of retail spaces and cubicles, but everything was stripped away now except for the walls and some light fixtures.

"How is this perfect?" Reco asked.

"You just need to have a little vision," I teased. I knew he had vision, but more often than not, he was held back by practical things like money and time. We still hadn't gotten out of the lease for my previous salon; according to the leaseholder, I still owed a ridiculous amount of money for a salon that wasn't even up and running.

So, when Reco looked at the space, he didn't imagine where the salon chairs would go or what the front desk would look like or where a large corner office with floor-to-ceiling windows would be. He simply saw a big, empty warehouse that was going to take a lot of money, effort, and time to fix up, while thinking about all the money still potentially tied up in litigation for the old salon. I swore that salon would haunt me for the rest of my life. I would be in a nursing home one day having nightmares about that damn place.

I understood. Given the facts, buying another giant space that needed massive renovations sounded crazy—and not a little naïve—and certainly not part of a savvy business plan. But despite the old salon fiasco, we were actually doing great financially. I hit a low point all those years ago when Rylan was stealing. I couldn't pay the bills, and I had no idea how I would ever claw my way back to the life I had once envisioned sitting at the bar at the NTR conference. I had taken a leap then by spending too much money to learn how to do extensions, and shortly after, I thought that leap would drown me and the salon. It almost did. It tried.

I can imagine some might think the moral of my story at that point should have been to stop taking risks. But I actually saw my experience in the opposite light. I learned to persevere. I could have given up. Maybe I should have cut my losses, found some other business, and walked some other path, but that wasn't me. I had goals, and I was going to reach them regardless of what tried to get in my way... including myself.

Yes, at times in my life, I was actually the biggest threat to reaching my own goals. I let myself believe what other people said about me. Way back before I had my own salon, I shuffled from one place to the next, and although I hate to admit it even to myself, there were moments I questioned whether I was good enough. Whether I would ever belong.

When I opened my own salon, the same self-doubt crept in. Maybe I couldn't manage money. Maybe I couldn't surround myself with the right people. Maybe I took too many risks. Those thoughts and insecurities played out time and again. They seeped in yet again when Rylan manipulated most of the girls I had hired into turning their backs on me and joining her. Maintaining a strong foundation when everyone around me wanted to break it down was difficult.

Speaking of Rylan's betrayal, I heard through the grapevine (the grapevine, in this case, was named Lacey) that Rylan and Izzy and the others were doing "all right." My imagination filled in the unspoken part: the other girls who had been duped by Rylan were probably starting to learn exactly what kind of manager and business owner she was. Standing in the open space that I hoped would one day be my high-end, fully customized salon space, I no longer cared what the hell happened to them. Maybe that was callous, but I had been burned too many times from too many directions. I didn't wish them well; I didn't wish them ill. I didn't wish them anything so long as it was far, far away from me.

Despite my previous struggles, standing in that warehouse that day, I had no doubts. I had managed to build a business from absolutely nothing, packaging products and stuffing envelopes on my living room floor surrounded by the most amazing people in my life, people who believed in me wholeheartedly. That business grew so big that Reco quit his job to manage it. I had grown HRH's mentoring program by making training videos and offering shadowing services. I now made enough that we didn't really have to worry about money. If I were to judge my life against the goals I made sitting at the NTR conference bar, I could easily claim victory. I had met those goals. I had my own business. I had made a name for myself in the community. I traveled all over the world.

It was time to set a new goal. I wanted to turn this warehouse of gray walls, concrete floors, and a few windows into a paradise of my own design. I wanted clients to walk in and feel like they had been transported into a luxury salon where I could meet all of their beauty needs. I wanted to use the space to grow Everything Hand Tied, so we didn't have to run it out of our house anymore. I wanted an office for everyone who worked for me. When I spun around, I didn't see the same space that Reco saw. I saw our future.

He must have seen something in my face because before I could even open my mouth to speak, he held up a hand. "I get it," he said.

I jumped onto him, giving him a hug. "I knew you would," I said. We put in the offer that night.

The following day our offer was accepted. I wasn't surprised, given the market for retail and office spaces in the throes of the pandemic. Once it was a reality, I felt a little overwhelmed; there was a lot to do. But I had my team, and together we would make it happen.

In my first salon, I let Rylan do a lot of the decorating. I asked her to design it because she had a good eye for aesthetics, but also in part because I didn't trust myself yet. I had just come from a group of mean girls telling me that I didn't "fit in" at their salon. So, in the back of my mind, I worried that if I trusted myself on the look of the place, it wouldn't "fit in" with other stylists or clients.

Now, however, I wanted to throw myself into the design of my new space. I don't know if it was that my confidence had grown, so much as that I didn't care anymore. I wanted to build a space for people like me, not people like Rylan and Izzy and all the others just like them. I started believing that I deserved a space that represented my own vision.

The first steps were to move some walls around, refloor, and repaint. Then I would have some real decisions to make.

CHAPTER EIGHTEEN

I sat down for HRH's weekly Zoom mentor meeting. While waiting for it to start, feeling more and more like the meetings were a giant waste of time, my leg bounced with excess energy. I wanted to be working on my salon space, checking orders with Everything Hand Tied, or, better yet, working with my mentees. I had so many plates in the air that sitting down for a Tuesday night meeting in which Abby reviewed things I already knew felt impossible to get through.

But I did it. I put on my happy face and sat through the meetings once a week, every Tuesday. An idea had been forming in my mind, but I had not voiced it; yet I couldn't seem to let it go. That Tuesday, I finally said something. As people were starting to log off at the end of the meeting, I waved my hand to get Abby's attention.

"Hey, Abby," I said.

"Hey, girl, what's up?" she replied. A few stylists stayed logged on to listen.

"I have been thinking about these Tuesday meetings. I think they are great, but we should start thinking about the next steps," I said. I had been with Abby from nearly the very beginning and so felt comfortable discussing the long-term plan with her. The other girls were "yes women," too afraid to upset Abby by stepping out of line and questioning how things were done.

Abby paused with her wide smile, staring at the screen as if she didn't understand what I was saying. "What do you mean? Next steps with what?"

"I mean, I don't think it's enough for everyone to just learn the method. There has to be a next step. There has to be continued education where we build on the method," I explained.

"We have the Tuesday meetings," she said. Moments like this showed Abby's inexperience. She hadn't been in hair and beauty long enough to understand the typical progression of large-scale education.

"There has to be more. We have to build on what stylists have learned and provide more education opportunities," I said. "Like a master's program. Stylists can opt in and get continuing education."

"Well, I guess it's something we need to start thinking about," Abby said.

In the end, Abby worked her magic, and I soon found myself with another top-tier stylist managing a twelve-week master's program that included both pre-recorded and Zoom classes. HRH charged stylists thirteen to twenty thousand dollars to participate. Given the large fee was on top of all the other fees stylists paid, we were under a lot of pressure to create a program that was worthwhile.

At the time, I didn't question taking on more work. My only goal was to further the company. If Abby succeeded, we all succeeded. I was part of the team. While I didn't have ownership in the company, I made a lot of money with HRH through mentoring, styling, and shadowing.

Like most things that Abby started, the master's program started off rocky, with me filming the pre-recorded classes in my living room with little editing and no graphics or supplemental materials. The results were amateurish videos with great information. Justifying the cost of the program was hard, given the unprofessional quality. I felt like we were both moving in the right direction and ripping people off at the same time. Still, I hung my hat on the information and experience I brought to the project. My Zoom classes weren't much better as far as quality goes, but I had been instructing long enough that I could command the "room" to make my classes engaging and interesting.

It wasn't until Abby started putting inexperienced stylists into top-tier positions like teaching the master's classes that I started really questioning what we were doing. These women were dedicated loyalists to the brand and to Abby, so they got points for that, and they fit the cookie-cutter mold of a typical stylist, but they were also greener than the owner herself.

On paper, hopping on Zoom and teaching twenty or so women about technique, marketing, color, and styling sounds easy. But in truth, twenty women in one Zoom quickly devolves into either chaos or absolutely boring drudgery. It all depends on the host. A host with enough personality can make the information interesting and maintain order. Alternatively, if a host isn't dynamic enough to keep everyone's attention, a moderator can help by taking questions and managing the chaos.

I decided to talk to Abby about the problem at my next hair appointment. (I had been flying to Utah to have her do my extensions, while discussing HRH business, every six weeks since that first test visit.) In preparation, I watched every last one of the Zoom master's classes, which we always recorded, and took notes on how we could improve. I recognized that the quality of the classes was an absolutely pivotal sticking point in our growth. We had to get the master's program right or our reputation would be soiled. When I showed up for my appointment, I didn't waste any time.

"We need moderators in those Zoom master's classes," I said as soon as I sat in her chair.

"What the hell are you talking about?" she asked. I blinked several times before collecting my thoughts.

"Have you gone back and watched any of your classes?" I asked, trying to keep the absolute astonishment and admonishment out of my voice.

"No," she said so flippantly that I had to take several breaths to keep from berating her. I couldn't believe that she charged what she charged and didn't even bother to do quality control.

"Well, I watched them all, and you need a moderator. Those classes are either dead or chaos," I said. "Let me moderate them."

"How can you do that when you have so much else going on?" she asked.

"Don't worry about that. You know me. When I care about something and am doing something I enjoy, I make time for it."

"What would a moderator even do?" she asked.

I spent the next thirty minutes explaining the plan that I had already devised for controlling the classes' tone, pacing, and questions. I thought moderating would be really fun. When I was done, she told me she would think about it.

Several days later, I got word that Abby had hired a videographer and the pre-recorded master's classes would be filmed in Utah. Going forward, I and other presenters had to fly ourselves to Utah on specific days to record. An even bigger gut punch was that Abby would be moderating the Zoom classes henceforth. I couldn't understand why she didn't take me up on my offer to moderate. I had shown I was good at navigating through dead space while educators presented live, whereas Abby, despite being present at every Zoom meeting, had never once controlled the space; she was all over the place. If it were a matter of her valuing loyalty over quality, I was still puzzled; I was as loyal as they came. I had joined early and dedicated everything to Abby's vision. I was offering to do more work without any extra compensation on her end. I just wanted the master's program to be successful because without it, the business stagnated.

Even after this latest blow, I didn't doubt the company, the mission, or Abby, but I was struggling to maintain a sense of self and purpose in the face of constant push-back. If I was just another cog in the wheel at some large, big-name brand, I would get it. But that wasn't the case. We were a small, up-and-coming, mom-and-pop shop. We weren't over-the-top glamorous like NTR nor were we small and disorganized like JLM. We were carving out our place as a personal brand that could be trusted. I very much thought of us as a "we."

Why, then, did it feel like I was sometimes on the outside looking in?

CHAPTER NINETEEN

In the weeks that followed, I let go of my frustration about HRH's takeover of my tutorial videos, shadowing program, and Zoom moderator idea and simply worked my ass off redefining myself and my goals. I continued to finish my already-booked shadowing sessions, create new mentoring videos, scale up Everything Hand Tied, and work on my new salon space. Every step of the way had been a gamble that was paying off. So, when I got a cryptic text from Abby one day while working in my new space, I had no idea how to respond.

I feel like I can't trust any of my mentors.

The bottom dropped out of my stomach. I had no idea what the hell she was referring to, but you can't read something like that and not have a visceral reaction. My many years in the hairstyling, coloring, and extension world conditioned me to live on high alert, waiting for drama. And this text sent an alarm bell clanging in my brain.

I read the text several times as I sat at the small desk in the little office that temporarily acted as our one-room control center, shipping department, and storage facility for Everything Hand Tied. I had already been up for several hours and had multiple cups of coffee in me, but still the words hardly made sense. I didn't have drama with Abby. Abby was chill and easy going. Abby valued me and my input.

"Maybe she is talking about her other mentors," I mused out loud. I knew the other ten mentors by name, even though I wasn't super close with all of them. I mentally scanned through them. They lived all over the country. Casey lived in New York City in a seven-hundred-square-foot apartment with her boyfriend. Janice was smart as a whip. Sue Ellen never had a mean thing to say about anyone. Brianna was a Utah native. She and a few others who lived in or near Utah were wrapped up in the Mormon culture, which was a lifestyle I found completely alien. I knew Abby was Mormon, which guided a lot of her beliefs, actions, and choices, but I didn't dig too much into it. As far as I was concerned, it didn't impact me. We all should be able to live our lives however we see fit. It wasn't until much later that I realized her being Mormon may have been a red flag.

After taking inventory of the mentors, I couldn't imagine what any one of them might have done that would lead Abby to distrust all of us. At the same time, I understood what stress could do to a person. Abby was growing a million-dollar company from the ground up. In the end, it was her brand and reputation on the line, and both were affected by what her mentors did. Still, I didn't appreciate the cryptic text, the not-so-subtle accusation, and the inevitable drama that would unfold. I had to respond, but I wanted to do so in a way that would limit the drama as much as possible. I thought about those movies full of misunderstandings, where one five-minute conversation early on would have prevented an entire conflict. Having the conversation early doesn't make for great cinema, but it really helps in real life.

What's going on? I finally wrote back. I wanted to get more information before I jumped in feet first.

Exactly what I said. I can't trust any of my mentors. You are all just in it for yourselves.

It was the use of the word *you* that really stung. So, this wasn't about one of the other girls. This was about me, too. What the hell did I do? I was tempted to text that as my response, but I remembered my no-drama rule and took a deep breath.

We need to have a conversation. Please call me.

Three typing dots popped up on my screen, and I nearly shouted. How did she expect to have this conversation over text?

I just can't trust any of you as far as I can throw you.

I could tell from how quickly she sent out the rapid-fire response that she was rage texting. I had a lot of choice words that I wanted to throw back. I wanted to remind her that I created the videos she was using; that I worked my ass off taking more clients than anyone else; that new mentees were requesting me by name. But I couldn't let myself be dragged into a text fight. She was clearly pissed off and wanted to vent, but her anger had no basis, and I didn't plan on being her punching bag. So instead, I replied:

I don't know what is going on, but if I am going to continue as a mentor, we need to have a conversation. Please call me.

Three more dots popped up momentarily before disappearing. When I stood up to leave and get some fresh air to clear my head, the phone rang.

"Hey, Abby, what is going on?" I asked upon answering.

"It's exactly what I said. I can't trust any of you." She wasn't shouting, but her tone was clipped, and I could feel the tension boiling just under the surface of her words.

"Why?" I asked, genuinely at a complete loss. I felt like I arrived in the middle of someone else's dream with no context for all of the crazy, nonsensical shit happening around me.

"I know that you all are trying to steal from me and take advantage of me. You know I gave all of you a chance. I brought you all in at the ground level and put you in trusted, high-level positions in my company only for you to use me and steal my hard work for your own gain. It is bullshit, Rachel, and you know it."

A few things about that got under my skin and made me feel itchy all over. First was the way she said, "my company." It *was* her company. I never once doubted that. But to hear her talk, you might imagine she was running a charity service and we were all freeloaders, which couldn't have been further from the truth. The second thing that bothered me was that she was still refusing to tell me exactly why she didn't trust me. Third, she was lumping me in with everyone else, even though I had worked tirelessly for her company. But what I hated most of all was that we had so quickly turned into enemies. Whatever happened, she had immediately jumped to the conclusion that I was against her. She didn't give me the benefit of the doubt. I liked to think that if the situation were reversed, and I heard some salacious or harmful rumor about Abby, I would assume the best about her before announcing that I no longer trusted her.

I had no idea how to respond. I tried to quickly process all my immediate gut reactions and collect my thoughts.

"I feel like we are the backbone of this company," I finally said. "There is no way that you could have grown the way you did without hardworking, loyal, and skilled mentors busting their asses training all the new clients. Whatever you heard can't possibly erase everything that we have done."

"It's not what I have heard, Rachel." She practically spat out my name. "It is what I know. You girls are trying to steal from me."

"Can you please just tell me what the hell happened?" I asked. It was getting harder and harder to keep taking the high road. I really wanted to maintain a calm, patient tone. My goal was to hear her out and support her, while also defending my position, but I couldn't do any of that without knowing what was really going on.

"You are going around telling all the girls they should use their positions as mentors with HRH to steal my ideas, take what they need, and use me and my company to benefit themselves!" She was much closer to shouting this time. I blinked several times and shook my head. I had never said anything like that.

"What are you talking about?" was all I could think to say.

"Exactly what I said, Rachel. Don't even try to deny it." She continued ranting, but I tuned her out as I tried to make sense of the accusation. Either someone was lying, or she had misunderstood. I parsed through my memories, looking for any conversations I had with other mentors that might be construed as me telling them to take advantage and steal. Abby was in the middle of a sentence when a thought came to me so suddenly that I couldn't help but interrupt.

"Oh!" I said. "I think I know what you are talking about. I was talking to Sue Ellen. She was telling me how much she was struggling to grow her salon, outside her mentorship. I told her that she should use the master's program to help network." To me, that was just run-of-the-mill good business advice. I imagine networking is one of the first things taught in any business school. "I told her how selling Everything Hand Tied hair in your store has really helped me and that she should think about similar strategies. Why do something alone when you can get help?"

"Exactly," Abby spat. "You are encouraging these girls to use me."

"Abby." I took a deep breath that probably sounded like an exhausted sigh. This was the exact kind of drama that could fester and destroy healthy working relationships. "I am sorry you are feeling that way. I believe wholeheartedly in HRH. I am on your side. I am a thousand percent committed to this endeavor."

As we continued to talk, it became clear that Abby's worries and anger were less about that one conversation with Sue Ellen and more broadly about her overall worries, stress, and paranoia. We spent three hours on the phone, each unloading our fears and worries, before finally coming back together as friends.

By the end of the three hours, the conversation felt like a warm hug, as much as a hug is possible from a great distance. Much like my vulnerable, honest conversation with Nica the first time we went to dinner together, my conversation with Abby started out contentiously but ultimately made me feel closer to her, and I hoped that her concerns were assuaged.

I meant what I said. I planned on being in HRH for the long haul. And when I hung up the phone, I felt even more committed to the brand and the vision, and even closer to Abby. I thought she felt the same.

CHAPTER TWENTY

At the tail end of 2020, I couldn't have been happier. In March, much like the rest of the country, I worried I wouldn't be able to survive a shutdown and the major up-heaval that followed. But somehow, the shutdown turned out to be the best thing that ever happened to me. It forced me to re-evaluate my situation, my priorities, and the company I kept. By the time December rolled around, I had cut out all the toxic people who had been holding me back; I had found a new space; Everything Hand Tied had nearly doubled in business, thanks to my collaboration with Abby and Ron; and I was the most sought-after mentor within HRH.

On December 31, Reco and I sat at a nicely catered New Year's Eve dinner with a handful of close friends. The atmo-sphere was relaxed and energetic at the same time. Everyone was happy to see the end of 2020, and although it turned out to be a great year for me, I, too, was looking forward to what 2021 might bring.

"So, what's your New Year's resolution?" Reco asked, sipping his beer and leaning in close. I didn't spend even a fraction of a second thinking about it.

"I'm going to have a million dollars in my bank account by the end of the year."

His eyes grew wide, and a smile spread across his face. "That's ambitious."

"That's what resolutions are for," I said.

"It's gonna be an interesting year," he smirked.

"I hope so."

I rang in the New Year full of hope and the promise of dreams to come. We were working on renovating our new space that would house my Urban Elements salon and the Everything Hand Tied offices and warehouse. Every time I walked into my tiny ten-by-ten home office, filled with too much product and people and papers, I felt like I couldn't possibly wait another second to move into the new space.

But we had big plans for renovation that couldn't be rushed. In my mind, that space was the last space I would ever need, and it had to be perfect. I wanted it to be modern, high-end, and classy, but most importantly, I wanted it to reflect me. I wanted to infuse every nook and cranny with my aesthetic style. There were moments, as I flipped through catalogues and browsed online retail vendors, when I questioned if I knew exactly what my style was. Those familiar doubts that plagued me and became engrained in my psyche during my salon-hopping years crept back in. Did I have my own unique style, or had I just picked up the styles and opinions of others that had been fed to me for so long? Then I would see a stylist chair or a beautiful piece of wall art and just know, deep in my gut, that the item belonged in my salon. It took weeks working with a contractor and interior designer to design the perfect concept for the space. As the renovations began, my idea to rebrand Urban Elements as much more than just another high-end salon started coming together. I wanted it to be everything, and there was no doubt in my mind that it could be.

Reco, Nica, and Sarah sat around my table that January for our monthly Everything Hand Tied meeting. Again, I couldn't wait to be in a real conference room with floor-to-ceiling windows and a large modern table where everyone had a comfy swivel chair, but until then, my dining room table had to suffice. We had already gone over budget reports, a necessary evil when running a business, something I had learned the hard way while working with Rylan. As painful as that experience had been, I could, at least in hindsight, appreciate everything I had learned from her betrayal. Without it, I wasn't sure if I would have been ready to take Everything Hand Tied as far as I did.

Part of the budget, of course, focused on how much revenue came from Abby's storefront and my affiliation with HRH, who maintained a steady monthly purchase of around fifty thousand dollars' worth of hair. I felt good about my heart-to-heart with Abby last month. It had been the right thing to do, from a friendship stance as well as a business stance, as the numbers showed—though it was hard to tell how the affiliation with HRH and additional press had specifically bolstered our sales.

I scanned through my hastily written agenda for the meeting. The one challenge of working with my best friends was the ease at which meetings devolved into casual chat sessions. Without the agenda, I had no hope of keeping us on track. "Are we ready for the Black History month sale?"

"In terms of inventory, we are good. I think we should have enough to meet the increased demand," Sarah said.

"Okay, good. I want the social media marketing ready to go well ahead of time. The sale starts on January 15, so we should be pushing out the announcements by the tenth." Black History Month wasn't until February, but as a team, we decided to start the twenty-percent-off sale on Martin Luther King Jr.'s birthday as a way of honoring our southern and black roots. The team confirmed we were good to go, and we concluded the meeting talking about the new space, my current favorite topic. I showed them the latest design sketches, and we all pored over them with equal enthusiasm. We never talked about it, but the truth was that getting that space was a huge accomplishment, making us feel like we had really made it.

I left the meeting feeling amazing. There was something so empowering about running my own business, being able to make decisions and highlight things within the culture that are important to me. I planned the social media for the sale carefully. Teasers would be posted leading up to the day of the sale, and then finally, on January 15, the sale would be launched. We had done plenty of sales in the past, and this one was no different, but like everything else related to my brand, my image, and my business, I would keep a close watch. I would monitor how the teaser posts performed and how many people visited our website. I wanted everything to go smoothly.

When I saw Nica calling on January 15, I assumed it was a routine call. We talked all the time. We talked about kids and husbands and business and vacations and ladies' nights and our favorite coffee and new shoes. But when I picked up the phone, I immediately knew something was wrong. We have a sort of best-friend telepathy that came through in the way we carried ourselves, said hello, or even breathed over the phone.

"Everything okay?" I asked.

"No," she said. I sat down, waiting for her to elaborate. Nothing could have prepared me for the words that came out of her mouth next. "Abby and Ron—HRH—they launched their own hair line."

"What?" I asked because I didn't think there was any way I could have heard her correctly.

"Yes! They launched their own line," she said. "They are pushing some bullshit top-of-the-line Scandinavian or European hair or something."

"What the fuck?" I shouted, probably too loudly, but my blood was boiling. I stood up and started walking in tiny circles around the room. I felt like I couldn't breathe. "I-I..." I stammered, unsure of what to even say. "How the hell could they do this?" I sat back down at my desk and pulled up all my social media, and there it was. HRH ads selling "premium" hair—even though no such thing actually existed; it was all just a PR stunt. A PR stunt that everyone who followed Abby would absolutely believe. Then I quickly navigated to the HRH website. I slumped back in relief. Despite the new launch, they were still selling my hair. "What do I do with this?" I asked.

"I don't know," Nica said. "They have put you in an impossible situation. If you confront them, they may cut ties all together. But if you don't, they will just keep taking advantage of you."

I knew what she said was true, but still, I couldn't imagine that those were the only options. I couldn't believe Abby and Ron would completely turn their backs on me. Abby and I were tight. I traveled to see her every six weeks to get my hair done. In fact, I had just been there, and no one spoke a word of this. They had to have been putting this launch into motion for weeks, if not months—and no one told me? That stung. I don't know what I would have said had they told me ahead of time, but being blindsided certainly didn't help the matter. Finding out through social media felt like an extra, purposeful stab in the back, as if they were trying to send me a message without having to say a word at all.

I didn't have to debate long on how to handle the situation. Later that night, Ron's name popped up on my phone's lock screen announcing his call. I hesitated for only a second, my stomach tied in knots as I wondered what the hell to say to him. "He is the one who has to apologize," I reminded myself. I stepped into my home office and answered my phone.

"Ron," I said, letting my tone speak volumes about my mood.

"Rachel," he said in the same tone of voice. I thought, What the hell does he have to be mad about? I opened my mouth to lay into him, but he jumped in before I could speak. "This is low, even for you."

I blinked several times, trying to catch up to a conversation that had, in one brief sentence, flown right over my head. Again, what the hell did he have to be pissed about? And why "even for me," as if I had a history of being anything but hardworking, kind, and supportive?

He continued. "I have been getting social media messages all day from the other HRH girls that you have been sending out blasts about your sale. The girls are not happy. They practically demanded that I get on the phone with you and make you cut it out. I truly cannot believe that you would start your sale early just to undermine our launch."

I felt like I had fallen into an alternate reality. I expected to pick up the phone and give Ron a piece of my mind for him and Abby going behind my back and starting their own hair line. He undermined my business, damaged our working relationship—which I considered a friendship, too—and now he had rolled out a product that was a direct competitor of

Everything Hand Tied, undoubtedly using the ten-year plan I had shared with him in detail the day he asked to sell my product at HRH. I expected him to act at least a little contrite, even if it was fake. I expected him to want to repair our relationship, to smooth things over again, even if it was with empty promises. That would have been a little better than nothing. But not only was he not apologizing, he was accusing me of damaging his business. He tried to paint *me* as the underhanded, sneaky one. I couldn't believe it. My jaw was on the floor. I could hardly formulate a sentence.

"What are you talking about? I didn't even know you were launching a hair line. But it sounds like your other girls knew all about it, and I was the only one left in the dark," I retorted. I could imagine the girls he was talking about. Abby and Ron had been slowly amassing HRH loyalists whose relationships with them went beyond working colleagues, beyond friendship, and even beyond devoted mentors and stylists. I might have fallen into those categories, but nothing like these girls. They were worshipping in the church of HRH. Their DMs must have been abuzz today, sharing my sale posts and shit-talking me.

"Maybe if you were more on board with HRH, rather than so focused on yourself and what you can get from us, you would know what was going on," he said, which sounded suspiciously like Abby's earlier complaint. They both seemed to think I was somehow untrustworthy. That I was so focused on my own personal gain that I wasn't a team player. That I didn't have HRH's interest at heart. Their line of thinking blew my mind. I had revolutionized how they mentored. I had single-handedly designed a shadowing program and then handed it over to them so they could profit from it. I had shared my strategies for Everything Hand Tied in depth, thinking they would be there with me every step of the way.

"Listen, we plan our sales a quarter ahead. Launching our sale today was not a last-minute decision," I said. "It is unfortunate that it came on the same day as your launch, but I really think you could have communicated better with me." I was seething, but I wanted to patch our relationship. I was still deeply entrenched in HRH, and, the truth was, I still wanted to be part of it all. HRH was the biggest thing happening in extensions, and after all the work I had done, I didn't want to be left behind.

"I think you should work on smoothing things over with the other stylists and mentors," he said. "Your relationships will become toxic if they think you are trying to undermine what we are all trying to build. And nothing good will come of that."

"Alright," I agreed.

Ron abruptly switched back to business as usual, as if nothing had happened. "We decided to put together a convention this summer. I would like you to work on programming for the elite members. I'll connect with you later on the details," Ron said in a cheery, enthusiastic, light tone of voice. A tone I thought was reserved for his close friends but appeared to be the voice he used to manipulate people.

"Okay," I said, not trusting myself to say anymore. I shook my head as we got off the phone. I ran through our conversation over and over and tried to figure out how I had ended up on the defensive so quickly. A familiar low-level anxiety grew just beneath my skin as I worried over what all of this meant for my relationship with Abby, Ron, the company, and the other girls.

Somehow, I had been thrust back into 2016, trying to please everyone around me without a clue how to do so.

CHAPTER TWENTY-ONE

"What the hell?" Reco's reaction was exactly as I had expected. He balled his hands into fists and stalked back and forth across the floor. He wasn't a reactionary kind of guy. He spoke in monotones most of the time and kept his emotions pretty well under wraps, but someone undercutting our business provoked a strong response.

"Do you think it's going to affect our sales?" Sarah asked. Gathering the Everything Hand Tied gang on short notice was tricky, especially since Nica ran an entirely separate business with her own husband, but after my call with Ron, I sent an urgent text, and an hour later four of us were sitting at my dining room table, trying to make sense of the news.

"It's hard to say," I answered. "I don't know what factory they are using. I never told them which factory we use, so it is unlikely that they happened to find the same one. I do know that they are marketing their wefts differently than ours. They are leaning hard into selling wefts from European donors, probably with a hefty markup for buyers too unaware to know better, while still selling Everything Hand Tied wefts. I'm sure they are trying to diversify."

"Well, they are doing it in a really gross way," Sarah said, and I couldn't have agreed more. Everything about it gave me the ick. They were flat out lying to customers about what kind of hair they were selling, and, of course, they did it all behind my back, which was entirely purposeful, no matter what Ron said.

"I guess there is a chance that things will continue, business as usual?" Sarah asked.

"I guess," Nica said, but her voice sounded as suspicious as I felt. "If they are willing to do this behind our backs, it makes you wonder just how trustworthy they are."

That wasn't a thought I wanted to consider. I truly, wholeheartedly believed that I had found my people in HRH. I had huge success with them and, in turn, brought success right back to them. My success as a mentor was directly tied to the success of the company. "It just doesn't make sense that they would want to undermine me somehow," I said. "How would that possibly turn out well for their bottom line?"

"It's impossible to know what they are thinking or what their long-term plans are. Right now, you still mentor, you shadow, we sell hair, and you need to prepare for the summer convention," Nica pointed out. "While I don't fully trust them, I agree it doesn't sound like they are cutting ties with us altogether."

"Maybe they are just too stupid to know how to manage people," Reco interjected, and I thought there might be some truth to that. I knew they weren't stupid in general. They had amazing marketing talent and had built up a giant business in a short amount of time, but they were very green. They had relied heavily on my input just about every step of the way. So, while I wouldn't use the word *stupid*, I might say *naïve* or *inexperienced*.

I just shrugged. It almost didn't matter. We had no choice but to forge ahead. I would work on the elite program for the convention, but I would talk one-on-one with Abby the next time I flew to Utah to get my hair done. I wanted to get her take on the secrecy behind their weft rollout.

After the emergency meeting, I drove to my new salon space. Although far from finished, it had become my happy place. I walked in and nearly squealed with delight at the latest additions. I wasn't a squealer by nature but seeing the rough stone wall where the reception desk would go pushed all thoughts of HRH right out of my mind. I walked through the building. The exposed beams above had been finished, giving it a cavernous feel. Reco and I had gone back and forth on that, trying to decide if we should go with a traditional sheet rock ceiling or keep the vaulted ceiling open. In the end, my gut told me to go with the latter. It made the place feel bigger, but it also matched my aesthetic. I had already ordered various chandeliers and cylinder lights that would hang down through the beams, and one of the walls had a red brick finish.

Although the place still needed a lot of work, it already felt like home.

I walked past the three-quarter wall that separated the salon space from the office space and found where I envisioned my desk going. I leaned up against the wall and let myself just exist for a few minutes, momentarily putting aside the overwhelming pressures pushing in from all around. I breathed deeply and let out a heavy exhale. I didn't know what to think of Ron and Abby. No one else on the Everything Hand Tied team had the relationship with them that I did. To Nica, Reco, and Sarah, they were just the people who bought our hair wefts. To me…well, I really thought they were like family, or at least really good friends. I believed with my whole heart that they understood me and, more importantly, saw real value in me. I hated the doubt I felt. I hated that I had to question my place with HRH and my friendship with two people who seemed so totally aligned with my goals and way of thinking.

I determinedly pushed thoughts about HRH out of my head. I had far too much to do to be sucked into any nonsense, and in the end, I had to maintain my perspective. I was their highest earner. Objectively, I had a lot of value in the company.

Over the next several weeks, my socials were abuzz about the new HRH hair line. I worked really hard to resist an eye roll every time I saw it mentioned. I think I did fairly well, too, until I saw how they structured its branding. Rather than launching the product as a fully owned and operated branch of their existing HRH business, they created a new company named Amabie and handpicked Casey, one of their most loyal (and from my perspective, most vulnerable) girls, to lead it. It was a thinly veiled way to make most of the profit while giving Casey a small percentage—thinly veiled to me, at least.

Casey joined HRH when she was quite young. She complained to anyone who would listen about her oversized bills and undersized income. I understood the complaint, especially in the past year. Wondering how to pay the bills during COVID lockdown was a stress I knew all too well. But in January 2021, it became clear Abby had been listening and recognized Casey's financial vulnerability. Suddenly, with the utmost care and guidance from Ron and Abby, Casey was the brand-new owner of her very own hair company. I had spent four hours describing my ten-year plan to Ron, as well as the ins and outs of what it took to build a hair company, thinking he wanted to be an investor. Instead, he delineated my plan word for word and transferred it to Casey to execute.

Again, I wondered why the hell working with Everything Hand Tied wasn't good enough. From the outside, HRH's relationship with Amabie looked like the exact same kind of setup they had with me. Casey's "company" bought and sold the products through a partnership with HRH, just like we did. The key differences that weren't obvious from the outside were control and, of course, money. Abby and Ron knew perfectly well that I would never hand over to them full control of my company, my baby, for them to manage as they saw fit.

I also would never hand over most of my profit, whereas as they could take advantage of Casey's inexperience and take a high cut.

I should have been mad at Casey for undermining me, but I couldn't bring myself to be upset at a young girl taking an opportunity presented to her. Later, I would even come to feel deeply sorry for her. She was roped into something with little growth potential that she had absolutely no control or say over.

Still, the whole ordeal needled me. When I confronted Abby at my next hair appointment, she tried to convince me it was "just business, love!" in her syrupy sweet way that I once was so drawn to and now just felt exhausted by. She brushed off my concerns that she went behind my back, pretending as if I just hadn't been paying close enough attention. She also assured me that HRH's relationship with Everything Hand Tied was just as solid as ever.

I tried to tell myself that their new hair venture was just business, as Abby insisted, but it wasn't just business to me. It was my life and my passion. It was my future and, in a lot of ways, my identity. Maybe it was stupid to invest myself to that extent, but I had been working toward my vision for so long that it was impossible to separate myself from what I did for a living.

CHAPTER TWENTY-TWO

The next blow came soon after the rollout of HRH's new hair line. It had been almost a year since I began shadowing clients with Abby's blessing; it had been about three months since Ron put an abrupt halt to it but assured me I could still shadow the clients I had already scheduled. He must not have realized that I had clients booked out for months in advance because he called again, fuming.

"Rachel, we need to talk," he said. As soon as I heard his tone, I couldn't help rolling my eyes and thinking, What now? I still felt like I was the one who had been betrayed in our relationship, yet he found a way to play the victim, as always.

"What's up, Ron?" I asked, trying to keep the frustration out of my tone, although he didn't make the same effort.

"I saw your Instagram post. Why the hell are you still shadowing? I asked you to put a stop to that," he said. "We are starting to roll out our own program, and you are still taking on clients."

"I'm not taking on new clients. I had that woman booked months out," I said.

"That isn't what we agreed to," Ron replied. That was, in fact, exactly what we had agreed to. Sometimes, the cracks in Ron's management ability were so obvious that I couldn't believe I had missed them before. He was easily overwhelmed.

"I'm not sure what to say, Ron. You told me I could keep the appointments I had already scheduled," I countered.

"You know, Rachel, this is really unfair to the other girls," he said, switching tactics.

"In what way?"

"They are all patiently waiting for their opportunity to shadow through the HRH channels, while you are just going off on your own and rubbing it in everyone's face," he said. It was all bullshit, of course—just another line about how worried he was about equity when actually he cared only about his bottom line. The other girls didn't care that I was shadowing. Ron cared that I wasn't falling in line with what he wanted; he didn't like me making money on my own, without HRH getting a cut.

I told him I understood but explained I had one last shadow commitment. "I can't cancel it. It has already been rescheduled twice due to Covid, my fee had been paid, and I've bought plane tickets."

A few months after that phone call, Ron sent a memo to all mentors outlining the HRH shadowing program he was putting together. It looked a lot like the program I had created, but, as I anticipated, it had more red tape: mentees were required to fill out a standardized form to request a mentor to shadow them. I worried it would turn into a clusterfuck. Ron also standardized the pricing, which was twice as much as I had been charging yet mentors would get several hundred dollars less because HRH's cut was so high.

I had mixed feelings about the price structure. The mentees were already paying through their teeth for the opportunity to learn, and all HRH provided were the three initial rounds of training videos. They relied on my stock videos for follow-up issues and questions, and they relied on the mentors to do the bulk of the training and teaching. I believed that if, as part of her training duties, a mentor wanted to go the extra mile to meet mentees and provide extra help, that should be between the mentor and the mentee. I didn't know if HRH deserved a cut, especially when it meant the mentor's cut was smaller than what I had been making.

I had never had to approach Abby or Ron with a grievance before, and I wasn't sure if I wanted to, let alone how to do so. But more and more, I felt a growing anxiety around my role in the company. It felt like the bottom was falling out. The shadowing program I built before Ron's interference was fantastic. It allowed me to travel, it allowed me to teach in person, and it brought in a lot of money. I really worried that the takeover might mess up any one of those positive things. I didn't want someone else to have their fingers in my relationships with my mentees. I liked being able to make my own schedule, to figure out the needs of my clients, to arrange to meet them without jumping through hoops. I liked being able to charge what I thought my time and effort were worth. But I was still a mentor for HRH, so there wasn't much I could do. I stayed quiet.

As the summer of 2021 rolled around, the HRH shadowing program was officially launched. My schedule booked up almost immediately. I was the most requested mentor for the new shadowing program, which wasn't a surprise to me, but Abby and Ron seemed unsure about why or how that happened. By then, our relationship had shifted. No longer was I the confidante whom they sought for business advice. I found myself on the outside looking in. It was an uncomfortable position to be in, especially after devoting so much of myself to helping Abby grow. She had built her business on the back of my emotional and physical labor, only to kick me to the curb when she no longer needed me.

I thought the "come to Jesus" conversation I had with Abby after she accused me of stealing from her for my own gain had ended on a good note. I thought it was a mutually understood moment of honesty and sharing between two queens, but I was starting to suspect that Abby was just making a play in a game I didn't know we were playing. Behind the scenes, she was planning and strategizing, moving pieces on her chessboard until the time was right. I didn't know this for sure, of course, but it was hard not to see the writing on the wall. The worst part of all was that HRH was using ideas and methods stolen directly from me to make choices that directly screwed me (and the other mentors) over.

That summer I could tell that Abby and Ron wanted to move me to a salaried position, or worse, they wanted to get rid of me altogether. You see, I was the only mentor still being paid a commission. The previous winter, HRH terminated every mentor who lived outside Utah (except me) and moved the Utah-based mentors to a salary-based system. I was no longer privy to HRH's behind-the-scenes decisions, so I didn't know the reason behind the mass firing, but I wondered if it was a Mormon thing. I didn't care what religion Abby practiced—to each his own—but the closer I got to her, the more I realized just how much Mormonism affected everything she did. Abby believed that entering the celestial kingdom depends partly on how much wealth one collects during life. She saw her place in heaven as having nothing to do with morality, just money. So, her goal at all times was to increase her bottom line; otherwise, she might find herself locked out of the celestial kingdom.

Despite the bad vibes I was receiving, I felt secure in my position mentoring and shadowing stylists. They couldn't let me go. It would have been a PR nightmare to fire their most requested mentor.

CHAPTER TWENTY-THREE

"Let me tell you all why I started this method." Abby spoke into a microphone from up on stage in front of the large group of convention attendees, all hanging on her every word. She had certainly gotten better at commanding a crowd.

It was October, and after eight months of planning, the "summer" convention had finally come together. Despite my hurt feelings and my suspicions that Abby no longer had my back, I moved forward with my work for HRH. I suspected they wanted to fire me, but we all silently agreed that they couldn't, and I wasn't willing to abandon everything I had worked to create at HRH; so, we were stuck together, which is exactly what it felt like. Gone were the warm feelings, replaced by worry and just a little resentment.

I found it interesting that Abby and Ron put me in charge of elite programming at the convention. It seemed at odds with their general demeanor and lack of trust in me. They must have recognized that I knew what I was doing. In the past, I probably would have been excited about the prospect of being in charge and the freedom to take the program in the direction I wanted, but by then, it just felt like more work.

The elite members, who eventually became known as Showcase Stylists, paid twenty thousand dollars to be on the short list of HRH's top stylists. The convention included the first elite training that would become an annual training required for keeping Showcase status. The idea for the entire thing—the convention, the training, the annual requirement—had come from a meeting I had with Abby before our relationship deteriorated. I told her in no uncertain terms that HRH had to start providing larger group training sessions for their stylists. While shadowing was helpful as extra training, none of the new members wanted to shadow, so it was not enough. I loved shadowing—working directly with other stylists was where I thrived—but I was only one person. I told Abby she needed to step up and expand HRH's training offerings. I tried to convince her that creating a larger reach and more opportunities for the elite artists was her responsibility.

Abby resisted the idea at first. She couldn't understand why no one wanted to shadow other mentors, or even herself. I don't think she wanted to spend her time training and teaching mentees individually, but she was the creator of the method, so it stood to reason that people would want to work directly with her. What she was missing was the amount of time, effort, and energy effective shadowing takes. It is not for everyone.

I gave each person I shadowed my all. I genuinely loved educating, and that came out in everything I did. Other girls went in with a one-size-fits-all approach and never truly understood their clients, whereas I saw my clients as unique individuals and addressed them as such. I tried to be the Mary Poppins of hair. I went into each session intending to pour a spoonful of sugar that would help them figure out not just the method techniques, but also their personal purpose and goals. Many of the girls I worked with wound up finding more genuine paths for themselves after our shadowing sessions. Sometimes that meant staying in the hair business and sometimes that meant something else entirely. What I provided simply wasn't the type of energy that could be bottled and passed out to other mentors to replicate. Abby didn't understand that I poured my soul into what I did while the other girls were chasing a paycheck.

Eventually Abby accepted that shadowing was not enough to fill the training gap, and she and Ron took my advice and planned the convention. (Maybe she did understand the passion and dedication I brought, at least a little, since they asked me to do the elite programming.) The convention had all the regular offerings you would expect to find, such as vendors, demonstrations, and classes, but it focused more on Abby's motivational speeches and a culminating party and award show. A lot of the stylists in attendance were die-hard Abby fans. They had drunk the Kool-Aid and were one hundred percent on board with whatever the convention had in store. I wondered, however, if some stylists were hoping for a little more in the education department and a little less in the worship-at-Abby's-feet department.

Abby booked the convention in a conference room at a swanky hotel along the California coast. It was an interesting bookend to that first NTR conference I attended. Back then, spending five thousand to attend a conference to learn a new extension method felt like a huge leap of faith. I had been a stylist almost my whole life and had never had to pay that kind of money for anything. Then suddenly, I was shelling out the big bucks just to walk in the door. It had been scary, but I sat at that bar, sipped my umbrella-adorned cocktail, looked out over the ocean, and set my intention. An intention that I had worked tirelessly toward ever since, regardless of setbacks. An intention that redefined how I saw myself and my work. Now there I was in another upscale California hotel, creating my own programs with HRH. While those earlier attempts at trying different methods didn't work out, they really validated the importance of that leap of faith.

My team from Everything Hand Tied manned a booth at the convention, so we could sell and network, but I was expected to be at Abby's side most of the time. I and three other HRH originals acted as Abby's entourage whenever she walked the convention floor, did photo ops, and mingled with the general public. She did not want to be approached by stylists without us acting as buffers. I can only guess at the reason; maybe she had anxiety, maybe she just didn't want to be bothered by the common folk. So, I spent the convention following her around unless she was up on stage, and even then, I stayed in the audience and watched her.

"I started this whole company," she continued to her rapt audience, "to get my pink Jeep. You see, my husband's software was doing pretty well, but every time I asked for a pink Jeep, he told me it was too frivolous. I knew I had to do something to get my own fun money!" The crowd cheered, and it took everything in my power not to gasp. Gone were the moving stories about independence, hard work, and girl power. In their place was a shallow anecdote about a pink Jeep. I couldn't believe that the people around me were buying into it. How could she get away with being so superficial and vapid?

Suddenly, I worried that HRH had been the wrong place for me all along. I had fallen for all of Abby's lines about helping other women, finding independence, and building a community. Were they all lies? Had she all along just wanted to line her pockets? No wonder her inner circle was shifting. I was a dying breed with my bleeding heart and my genuine desire to help my students. I thought Abby didn't realize that the new people she had been bringing in were chasing a paycheck, but it seemed now that she was one of them. Her speech left a bad taste in my mouth, which only got worse as the convention progressed.

"What did you think?" Abby asked when she came offstage, her eyes shiny with excitement. "I think they really liked it."

"It sounded like they did," I said, unable to lie outright about what I really thought of her message in the opening presentation.

"This was such a great idea. I'm so glad we are doing this convention. The energy is amazing!"

"It is!" I said. At least we could agree on that. "I am going to head off and get started with the elite program for the Showcase Stylists. I want to get everything set up."

"Oh, no. Didn't I tell you?" Abby asked, stopping to look at me.

"Tell me what?"

"We gave the Showcase Stylists to Diane. She is going to manage that so you can stay with me," Abby said. Her smile didn't falter as I gaped at her. She employed her usual strategy of acting dumb, as if she had no idea that I would be pissed about the change of plans. I had spent months prepping the Showcase Stylist portion of the convention, just for her to hand it off to one of her new minions. I wanted to scream or curse or simply walk out, but I knew just as well as she did that leaving wasn't an option for me at that time; I was too deep in to quit. We were stuck together, and it seemed she was trying to make it as miserable for me as possible.

I gritted my teeth and got through the rest of the convention feeling like an outsider yet again. It was a strange, disconnected feeling. Once, Abby and her brand had been my whole life. I didn't know where Abby ended and Rachel began. Now I couldn't help but think about how to separate myself, so I could be my own person again. I wondered how I could get back to my own growth and goals. The people I thought would save me from the catty pitfalls of the beauty world had turned into the worst perpetrators of all.

At the award show at the end of the conference, I sat in the audience at a round, white-cloth-covered table with the three other founding member stylists. On stage, Abby stood in front of four gold-plated records. Those awards had to be for the four of us; we had been integral to her success. Without us, and me specifically, no one would have been in that convention hall listening to Abby speak. I took some comfort that she would at least be recognizing me. It sparked just a little hope that my relationship with her and possibly even my place in the company could be salvaged. I hated the idea of starting over or burning my bridges. I had dumped so much of my time, energy, ideas, and myself into the brand that I still really wanted to be there, to see it succeed. Getting acknowledged for all my work would be all I needed to feel better.

"Now, what we have all been waiting for!" Abby said with a little excited squeal. "The awards! The first award for most growth in HRH goes to..." she paused, and I couldn't help but smile. "Lila Rainer!"

Once again, I found myself speechless. Lila wasn't one of the founding members at my table. She had been with HRH for only a couple of months. My stomach turned sour as I shared a look of horror with the other girls I sat with. That feeling only grew as Abby passed out the next award for "Best Color Work" to another new stylist. She wasn't going to acknowledge us. It was a slap in the face that left me uncertain of everything I thought I knew and wanted.

CHAPTER TWENTY-FOUR

As I headed home with my Everything Hand Tied team after the convention, a strange emptiness washed over me. I couldn't ignore the writing on the wall that my time with HRH was coming to an end, but what did that mean? Unlike when I was let go from Hogs and Heifers before opening my own salon, I had lots of things to keep me busy and help me feel a sense of purpose. My whole identity was not wrapped up in HRH—but enough of it was to still leave me feeling lost.

For the time being, I had to stay the course. I had put a tremendous amount of time, effort, and passion into growing the business...someone else's business. Thinking that all of that meant nothing felt like a punch in the gut. It was more than just the hurt over Abby's disregard for my work. It was that I had once again let my own needs become overshadowed by someone else's dream. Getting wrapped up in someone else's vision, especially one that presented such a strong, clear picture of success, had been so easy. I had felt certain that HRH was my ticket to the next big thing. In a way, it had been, just not in any way I could have possibly predicted.

The more time that passed after the convention, the wider my eyes opened to the truth that I had been blinded to for far too long. With a fresh perspective, I started noticing all the flaws in Abby's business model. More and more, I saw it for what it was: pay to play. Pay to get certified, pay to stay certified, pay to get more education, get paid to bring more girls in (like those pyramid schemes everyone warns you about).

Still, Abby didn't seem to have a problem using my ideas whenever it suited her, which was all the time. Her latest move was implementing my idea to train new stylists in person instead of with videos. She opened an education center in her hometown and held the first in-person certification class. Of course, she asked yours truly to design the curriculum and be the instructor. Three weeks after teaching the first class, I was sitting at the airport with Reco waiting to board our plane to New Orleans when my phone rang. Abby's picture popped up on the screen.

"Hey, Abby," I said. I had no idea what she was calling about, but lately, every time we spoke, I felt an anxious knot growing in my stomach as I waited for the other shoe to drop. I knew my value. I knew that HRH wouldn't be anywhere close to where it was had I not given them my ten-year plan for marketing wefts; had I not given them guidance on mentors, shadowing, conventions, and continuing education; had

I not developed the elite stylist programs. Yet, every time she called and I picked up the phone, I felt like some stupid kid waiting to be sent to the principal.

"Rachel, hi," she said, and I knew from her tone that I was right to be worried. "Listen, babe, this isn't going to be easy to say, but we need to let you go as a mentor." I felt the first warm tears squeeze from my eyes. This was extreme.

"What are you talking about?" I asked, trying to hold it together. I must have misheard her. I was their most popular mentor. I had started the whole damn program. They couldn't possibly take that from me.

"Sweetie, you are just too valuable. We can no longer pay you what you deserve. It just makes sense that we find another place for you in the company," she said. My throat threatened to close up with emotion. Her words dripped with saccharine lies. Her promise to find me a position more worthy of my talents was a backhanded compliment to make the conversation easier for her. I didn't argue or freak out. Luckily for her, I was stunned into silence as full-body sobs shook me. I could feel the eyes of the other airport patrons on me, probably assuming I was fighting with Reco. "Of course, we still want you to shadow. You are such an asset to us. We just have to find the right place for you."

I could barely get any words out. If I let myself read between the lines to the eventual end point of this conversation, I might have a meltdown in the airport. So, I got off the phone as quickly as I could and cried all the way to New

Orleans. It felt like the beginning of the end, or maybe it had been doomed from the start. Maybe a person like Abby and a business like HRH never saw me as a person, but instead as an asset to be used until there was nothing left to take.

I waited patiently for Abby to find another place for me. I continued to shadow my clients, put in my time, and be the good little employee I knew they wanted me to be. It only took a few months to get the text I had been dreading.

I had just sat down with Reco at a nice restaurant for his birthday when the text came through. He knew who it was the second I began reading it. My face gave away the panic that overwhelmed me.

I heard you have been talking shit about me in my own home! We need to talk right now! it read. Abby was still finding ways to surprise me.

"I have to call her," I said, holding up the phone to show Reco the text.

"Rachel, you have given your soul to those people. You work yourself to the bone for them to turn around and not appreciate you. This is the first time we are sitting down together in months. If you answer that text, we are going to have a problem," he said. He didn't say it like he was angry at me. He said it like he could have driven over Abby with a car without batting an eye. "You have spent three years at their beck and call. They say jump and you say how high. It is my birthday."

It took all the strength I had to text her back saying I was busy. It was ridiculous how hard not obeying her was.

Somehow, I had allowed Abby to manipulate me and play with my emotions for so long that I found myself always walking on a tightrope to keep her happy. She was like an abusive partner.

I want to talk to you by 8pm tonight, she wrote back.

"You will not," Reco said, shaking his head. "There is nothing she has to say that is that urgent. She can wait. Tell her which hours you are available during your business day. You have to set a boundary, Rachel. Abby and Ron have proven that they are not your friends. They do not get to interrupt every second of your life with their shit."

I took a deep breath and sent the text he suggested before putting my phone away and doing my best to enjoy dinner. When the meal was over, I saw I had missed several calls and texts from Abby, as well as a handful from other stylists in the program. I didn't even want to unlock my phone to read the messages. Abby was clearly having an epic meltdown about having to wait a few hours to talk to me, and I wanted to put off dealing with the fallout as long as possible.

I couldn't avoid it forever, though, so once we got home, I started scrolling. Abby certainly was having a temper tantrum. She had essentially erased me from HRH as if I never existed. I didn't appear anywhere on the website or social media. She removed me from all their accounts, blocked my access from classes that I had paid for, removed me from the shadowing program, and even took me off the list of HRH-certified stylists.

Friends I still had within the program texted me asking what was going on before sending me screen shots of the Facebook group posts. Abby, the woman I had considered a close friend for three years, who still regularly did my hair, whom I had looked up to and admired and appreciated, had spent the few hours of Reco's birthday dinner spreading nasty gossip about me. Through several posts, she spun my three years of work and dedication into a fantasy in which she was the victim and I was a selfish asshole out to get her.

I could only hope that the people who knew me recognized her hateful tirade as lies, but so many of the new stylists believed everything Abby had to say. She had replaced the thoughtful stylists she had originally recruited with an army of loyalists who lined up to revel in my downfall simply because she told them to.

It was finally over. My relationship with Abby, my position in the company, years of hard work. All over.

HRH had taken all of my ideas, all the knowledge and experience I had, only to turn around and get rid of me like I was a replaceable cog in a machine, a step on Abby's ladder. What I thought had been a place I could flourish as my true, authentic self, a place that had the opportunity to save me, turned out to be just another soul-sucking, self-serving business meant to use me up and spit me out.

In truth, as much as I hate to admit it, my time with HRH was a necessary step in my journey that started the day I was fired from Hogs and Heifers. Once again, I had trusted blindly, given myself fully. It wasn't my fault that Abby turned out to be a terrible person. It's possible that she was always that person and just good at hiding it, or maybe she had slowly shifted into an insincere, cutthroat, money-minded person over time. Regardless, my time with her had taught me about myself, my goals, my passions, and, most importantly, what was important to me. Perhaps without the challenges I faced at HRH, I wouldn't have been ready to stand on my own two feet without the comfort of someone else's capital, brand, and ideas behind me.

Back then, I thought I needed to be part of something bigger than myself to find my purpose, to have validation, to take my goals as far as they could go. I wasn't ready to see that I didn't need to hop on someone else's bandwagon. I had spent half my life hiding behind other people's ambitions, convinced I simply wasn't enough to stand on my own. Even when I opened Urban Elements, I thought I needed someone else to support my vision. I thought I couldn't do more than be the woman behind the chair. When Abby stole my ideas and broke my heart, I realized I had been selling myself short all along. I had been chasing her dreams while convincing myself they were mine, too. I had put on blinders because I wasn't ready to step out on my own.

In an amazing turn of events (that Abby would likely hate if she knew), her tearing me down actually had the opposite effect than she intended. It forced me to build myself back up. It allowed me to reclaim myself, to forge ahead, to find my identity without anyone else defining my purpose or passion. The beauty world, especially HRH, was clouded by petty dramas designed to make me feel superficially important but really just trapped me and dimmed my light.

As time passed and enough space grew between myself and my experience with Abby and HRH, I was able to breathe more easily, really breathe for the first time in a long time. I was no longer sitting by the phone waiting for Abby's approval. I found a new lease on life. I was no longer giving away my value to make other people money. I had the mental energy and wherewithal to focus exclusively on my own vision, to follow my own passions, and to follow my own lead. My only goal was to surrender to my yin energy, the feminine divine. To stop trying to mold myself into the model of a white, male-dominated, corporate world. To fully accept the space and energy that was uniquely my own while letting go of anything that no longer served me. I was done giving anything away. I was ready to keep some for myself while doing everything I could to help others shine.

In November 2020, I settled my lawsuit against the leasing company of my old salon; I was absolved from paying any back rent. In November 2021, I opened the doors to my new space. I decided against keeping the Urban Elements name after all, since Rylan had chosen it, and instead selected a name that embodies who I truly am and reflects the energetic vibrations I shine into the universe: The Sacred Hive Salon. The Sacred Hive is a very grounding place for me, for all who work there, and for all our clients. It is a place you can feel safe and seen as loudly or as discreetly as you choose. A place where you can release anything that does not fit or serve you. A place to connect with your own true self and vibrate off your own rhythm.

When I was finally confident enough to keep my talents and ideas for myself while doing everything I could to help others shine, I found the success and happiness I'd been looking for.

CHAPTER TWENTY-FIVE

Writing this book as I was recovering from the HRH drama was a cathartic experience for me. It can be tempting to look at events in your life and feel like a victim. Was I Abby's victim? Maybe, sure, in some ways. Did I also make choices that left me vulnerable because I wasn't ready to stand on my own yet? I think that's also true.

When I was first asked to leave Hogs and Heifers, I was hurting from a lifetime of not fitting in. But more than that, I had internalized the ideas that others placed on me. I had accepted the narratives from other people's stories and played the parts they created for me. Through all the experiences explored in this book, I was giving myself away, thinking that was the path toward self-actualization. Abby and Betty and all the others didn't have to take anything from me forcibly because I willingly gave it. I believed if I just gave enough and did enough that I would be enough for them, for the life I wanted, for the life I knew I deserved but didn't know how to reach. I looked to others to validate my ideas, my efforts, and my existence, so I didn't have to do the hard work of doing that for myself.

It was only through living the experiences I did, surviving the shit shows, and getting through the storms that I was able to recognize what I really needed. It wasn't money, or power, or even my own salon. What I really needed was to walk in my own true self and trust that I was enough. I had to trust that I already had the power within me to be everything I ever wanted. I didn't need people who fit a particular mold or stereotype that society deemed valuable to tell me where I stood. I built my own empire from the ruins of blind faith and the good intentions of others by putting my ego aside and accepting the lessons that life wanted to teach me. To that point, my next book will focus on how to be your own champion.

If you, my reader, take only one lesson away from this book, it is this: **Don't give yourself away**. There will always be people looking to take advantage of your work. They are practiced at convincing you that you need them to really thrive. Do they suck for trying to do that? Yes, of course. But don't let them get away with it. They can only prey upon people who are willing, and they only want to prey upon people who are valuable. Rather than letting others suck your value dry for their own gain, hold it close like the precious commodity that it is.

These are lessons easier said than done. My natural tendency is to believe the best of people, and while I have not fallen into cynicism, I now make sure that I get "paid first" both metaphorically and literally. It took me years to recognize the subtle, insidious ways people tried to take advantage of me, whether intentionally or unintentionally. Some people who try to take without giving are conniving and underhanded; others are simply focused on their own growth without considering the impact on others. With that type of person, valuing yourself is even more important. You must know your worth and make your growth a priority in a way that is sustainable and positive.

I'm still learning. I am always learning. But the difference now is that I understand the control I have. I recognize how to set clear, healthy boundaries both personally and professionally. I know how to trust myself and value my own goals and opinions without input from others.

My goal in sharing my story is to lift others up through mutual support in a way that I so desperately could have used on my journey to self-actualization. I hope to impart the lessons I learned from weathering the storms so maybe you won't have to go through the same things. Better things are out there for you, but first you have to know yourself, trust yourself, and value yourself. It wasn't until I accepted my own worth that I started seeing genuine success beyond what others were willing to dole out to me.

I am worth it, and so are you!

ABOUT THE AUTHOR

Rachel Nixon is the mother and creator of Mixed Methodologies, a hand-tied extension method. She is founder and CEO of Everything Hand Tied, a leading seller of hair extensions, and The Sacred Hive Salon, a transformative beauty and wellness sanctuary in Petaluma, California. An elite hair extension specialist and colorist for all textures, she has mentored more than 6,000 stylists on their own creative journeys for over 20 years. Embracing both her Black and Jewish heritage, she specializes in helping others visualize and then become the best versions of themselves.

To learn more about Rachel and Everything Hand Tied, please visit www.everythinghandtied.com.